IMAGES OF ENGLAND

SMETHWICK

PATENT
GRATES

TELEPHONE.
SMETHWICK 1251
(3 LINES) P. B. Ex
TELEGRAMS :
FORESIGHT GRATES
SMETHWICK

"GRATES WITH A DISTINCTION AND PURPOSE"

SAMUEL SMITH & SONS LT.D SMETHWICK

TELEPHONE: SMETHWICK 1181 (5 LINES)

TANGYES LIMITED

CORNWALL WORKS
SMETHWICK
BIRMINGHAM

LONDON
60 GROSVENOR ST, W
PHONE
MAYFAIR 1337/8/9

MANCHESTER
5 CROSS STREET, 2
PHONE : BLA 5320

GLASGOW
12 WATERLOO ST. C.2
PHONE: CEN. 6368 & 6369

CS 15339

YOUR REF.

TELEGRAMS
TANGYES
BIRMINGHAM
MANUFACTURERS OF
SPECIAL PURPOSE
MACHINERY
GAS OIL AND STEAM
ENGINES
STEAM AND POWER PUMPS
ELECTRIC PUMPS
COMPLETE INSTALLATIONS
HYDRAULIC MACHINERY
LIFTING TACKLE, CASTINGS
GARAGE EQUIPMENT

44715

OUR REF.

TELEGRAPHIC ADDRESS:
EVEREDS, BIRMINGHAM

A.B.C CODE 6TH & 7TH EDITIONS
BENTLEY'S

ESTABLISHED 1809

TELEPHONE No
SMETHWICK 0881

REGISTERED TRADE MARK

SURREY WORKS,
SMETHWICK.

London Office
MARCOL HOUSE
293 REGENT STREET
LONDON·W·I

Directors
J. H. WILSON
H. E. WILSON
E. A. WILSON
E. T. MILLER
H. ANDERSON
A. S. HARRIS
H. G. WILLIAMSON
A. H. WILSON

REFERENCES
YOURS | OURS

GH/FJ. Dept.4.   13th October 1939.

IMAGES OF ENGLAND

SMETHWICK

ANDREW MAXAM AND DAVID HARVEY

TEMPUS

Frontispiece: Three letterheads from some prominent Smethwick industries of the 1930s: Foresight Grates were made by the stove manufacturer Samuel Smith & Sons Ltd at the Beehive Foundry in Brewery Street, which was destroyed in an air raid in 1940 along with their shop on the corner of High Street and Rolfe Street. The world-famous hydraulic engineering company of Tangyes in Cornwall Road was built on the site of Rabone Hall. The Surrey works of Evered & Co. were located in the brass foundry area between the old Birmingham Canal and Lewisham Road from 1866. They were brass founders and tube manufacturers, first established in 1809. (A. Maxam Collection)

First published 2007

Tempus Publishing Limited
The Mill, Brimscombe Port,
Stroud, Gloucestershire, GL5 2QG
www.tempus-publishing.com

British Library Cataloguing in Publication Data.
A catalogue record for this book is available from the British Library.

ISBN 978 0 7524 4199 3

Typesetting and origination by Tempus Publishing Limited.
Printed in Great Britain.

Contents

Acknowledgements

The authors are grateful to the many photographers, both those acknowledged in the text and others unknown, who have contributed to this volume. Special thanks are due to Peter Drake of Birmingham Central Library for his invaluable assistance. Also thanks to Samantha Goode and colleagues at Smethwick Library. Other thanks are due to Chris Ash; Mary Bodfish; David Buxton of Tempus Publishing; David Bryant MBE; Steve Cemm; Carl Chinn OBE; Tony Usherwood of Sidney Darby & Son Ltd; Kieron McMahon of www.midlandspubs.co.uk; the family of the late Arthur Mumford; Mark Norton; Arnold Peace; Terry Price; Alan Reynolds; the late Joe Russell; South Staffordshire Water plc and finally Neil B. Todd, co-author of *Staffordshire Tavern Checks.*

Andrew Maxam, *Smethwick*
David Harvey, *Dudley*
August 2006

Introduction

Smethwick was once a small township within the ancient parish of Harborne to the west of Birmingham in the county of Staffordshire. The boundary between the townships followed the Birmingham-Halesowen Road. In 1831 the population was 2,676 and with industrial expansion and the coming of the railways it had increased to 54,539 by 1901. Smethwick became an urban district in 1894, a borough in 1899 and a county borough in 1907. In 1901 the borough had an area of 1,929 acres and was enlarged to 2,496 acres in 1928 by the transfer of Warley Woods from the urban district of Oldbury in Worcestershire ensuring Smethwick was one of the most densely populated county boroughs in England. In 1966 it was integrated into Warley, which itself became part of Sandwell MBC in 1974.

Smethwick, a name meaning the Smith's dwelling, is situated on the South Staffordshire Plateau. The geological formation is mainly Triassic sandstone overlaid with Pleistocene boulder clay. The highest ground is in the south and west reaching 753ft in Harborne Road, dropping to 421ft at Black Patch Park to the north-east. It is through the lower ground in the north that the canals and railways run leading to them becoming magnets for the development of heavy industry. The undulating ground had several streams, now largely culverted, flowing through the valleys and draining into the Tame Valley. These streams formed the boundaries at Hockley, West Smethwick, Spon and Thimblemill.

Smethwick was a thinly populated rural area, and in 1675 it was described as 'a discontinued village' scattered along the Birmingham-Dudley Road. The cutting of the Birmingham Canal in 1768-9 brought some industrial development, and a sharp rise in the population of the township to 1,097 in 1801. From the later eighteenth century, a number of Birmingham business and professional men came to live in Smethwick.

The number of industries continued to increase, above all with the opening of Telford's new canal in 1828. The first large industrial works was Smethwick Brass Works, in existence by 1790 (hence Brasshouse Lane) and in the same area was the development of bedstead manufacturing. In 1795, Boulton, Watt & Sons bought land by the canal near to the firm's Soho Manufactory in Handsworth; in 1796 they opened their Soho Foundry 'for the purpose of casting everything relating to our steam engines'. A mint was also established by Boulton. The foundry site was developed by the sons of Matthew Boulton and James Watt. In 1895 the site was bought by W. & T. Avery Ltd of Birmingham to make weighing machinery, who still occupy the site.

Many firms became engaged in engineering and metal trades using locally produced minerals found in the Black Country which could easily be transported by canal and later rail. Originally founded in the 1840s, Fox, Henderson of the London Works in Cranford Street became one of the most celebrated national civil engineers, famed for their work on the Crystal Palace in Sydenham, London. Tube-making firms such George Selby's Birmingham Patent Iron and Brass Tube, Smethwick Tube in Rolfe Street, Richard Evered & Co. and Credenda also became well established.

Birmingham Railway Carriage and Wagon Co. was one of the largest employers in the town, extending their premises over the border into Handsworth. Tangyes at their Cornwall Works pioneered hydraulic engineering, but later diversified into manufacturing steam, gas, petrol and oil engines. In the 1810s, the British Crown Glass Co. was formed, located by the Birmingham Canal just west of Spon Lane, and became Chance Brothers who began production in 1832 and pioneered the introduction of sheet glass as an alternative to crown-glass. Chance's sheet glass was used for Joseph Paxton's Crystal Palace in 1851. The company was later taken over by Pilkington's of St Helen's and was finally closed in the early 1980s, but the Spon Lane listed buildings still stand. Stained glass was made by Thomas William Camm at his purpose-built studio in High Street. During the later nineteenth century the manufacture of nuts, bolts, and screws became the town's most important industry and Smethwick emerged as one of the country's leading centres of this trade. The two largest firms, Watkins & Keen and Nettlefold & Chamberlain, merged in 1902 to become Guest Keen & Nettlefold. By the outbreak of the First World War they produced over half the screws and about a quarter of the nuts and bolts made in the country. The amalgamation made the firm the largest employer in Smethwick. Other industries in Smethwick were Doulton's pipe works, Ruskin pottery works at Oldbury Road; Titus Mason's soft drinks at Grantham Road and British Pens Ltd at Bearwood Road.

In the 1830s there was a brewery on the corner of High Street and Brewery Street run by one Thomas Robinson. The Smethwick Brewery in Oldbury Road was run in the early 1840s by Joseph Morris. Of greater significance was Henry Mitchell, licensee and brewer at the Crown Inn, Oldbury Road, who moved to a large site at Cape Hill and began brewing there in 1879 as Mitchell & Co. He formed in 1898 Mitchells & Butlers with William Butler which became one of the largest breweries in the country.

Immigration to this area for work is not new. Chance's brought French and Belgians to the glassworks in 1832. Subsequently Russian Jews, Poles and Irish settled in Smethwick and since the 1950s many more immigrants have arrived, including Indians and Punjabi Sikhs, Pakistanis and West Indians. It continues to be an ethnically diverse community today, with recent immigration from Eastern Europe.

one

Dudley Road
to Soho

Above: Two buses work their way into the city on the B82 service from Bearwood on 24 October 1964 in Dudley Road, just past the Lee Bridge Tavern on the corner of Heath Street. The leading bus is 2769, (JOJ 769), a Daimler CVD6 with a Metro-Cammell H30/24R body and is followed by 2230, (JOJ 230), a particularly handsome-looking Leyland 'Titan' PD2/1 with a Park Royal H29/25R body. The leading bus is passing over Lee Bridge which carried Dudley Road over both the Birmingham Level of the Birmingham Canal Navigations canal and the Stour Valley railway line between Birmingham and Wolverhampton. Overlooking this deep cutting are the rows of mid-Victorian terraced houses which were built on what had been Birmingham Heath. (W. Ryan)

Below: The one-and-a-quarter mile long Soho tram service across the Birmingham boundary into Smethwick was opened by the Birmingham & Midland Tramways Company on 31 December 1904 as far as the city boundary and was extended to Soho Station on 24 May 1905. Taken over by Birmingham Corporation Tramways on 1 July 1906 when the Company leases within the city boundary on the Bearwood and Heath Street services expired, the 31 tram service and all the Dudley Road tram routes was operated from Rosebery Street depot. Tram 89, a former Radial-truck car built in 1906 by UEC, turns off Dudley Road at the impressive Arts and Crafts-style Lee Bridge Tavern on 30 September 1939, the final day of operation for the Dudley Road trams. Beyond it are the grim-looking three-storied terraces and courtyards of Heath Street. There are sandbags on the pavements and an ARP Shelter sign in Dudley Road, showing that this was recorded in the early days of the Second World War. (L.W. Perkins)

A Metro-Cammell-bodied Daimler CVD6, 2767, (JOJ 767) in Heath Street working towards Winson Green Road on its way into the city on the B83 route, *c.* 1963. These 'New Look' fronted buses always used a single-track display in the destination blind in order to show the route number as the top number box did not have letters on the right-hand destination roll. This bus service had replaced the 31 tram route to Soho Station on 1 October 1939 and ran the length of the mid-Victorian back-to-back and terrace-lined Heath Street. Before crossing into Smethwick it became Cranford Street. The B83 service was always operated by the Corporation's Rosebery Street garage. Rosebery Street's allocation of twenty of these Daimler CVD6s entered service between December 1951 and March 1952. (A.D. Broughall)

Morley's newsagents and grocers shop was at the junction with Alma Street and Cranford Street. It was a typical back street 'hucksters' which sold everything from Brooke Bond tea to Aspros and Walnut Tobacco, *c.* 1963. Beyond the parked 1959 Ford Thames 305E van towards the Old Crystal Palace Inn, a Ford V8 Pilot comes down the hill, passing the waste ground on the left which until only recently had been occupied by terraced housing. The London Stores public house at the junction of Oakfield Road and Soho Street is just to the right of the bus stop. (Joe Russell)

Left: Looking towards the city in 1963, Cranford Street with the Old Crystal Palace Inn on the left and Soho Street off to the right. The area looks about ready for redevelopment. (Joe Russell)

Below: The Moilliets Arms and London House was at 49 Cranford Street at the junction with Moilliet Street. Mentioned in a directory of 1851, the pub was named after Jean Louis Moilliet, a Swiss merchant who sold part of his Smethwick Grove estate to provide a site for the London Works, an engineering company which was later involved in the Crystal Palace project. (M&B Crown Archive)

The London Stores pub, originally a Cheshire's hostelry, still trades today, with many of its original 1960s features intact, at 27 Soho Street near to the junction with Oakfield Road, Six Ways. The pub closed in 1966 during complete redevelopment of the area and the subsequent construction of the new Soho Way. The licence was transferred to the London Apprentice on 27 June 1969, a new pub which was built nearby at Soho Place. (Sidney Darby)

Turning from Soho Street into Cranford Street on the last day of tram operation on the 30 September 1939 is BCT tramcar 73. On the left is the Mitchells & Butler's Old Crystal Palace pub, known locally as The Copper Top because of the dome on the roof. The Bon Café on the right catered for 'Transport Men' with eggs and bacon for 6d and cups of tea and seems to have been sponsored by Craven A cigarettes! The 31 route terminus at Soho Station is just visible in the distance. Car 73 was one of the nineteen trams of the 71–220 class which were stored throughout the war years in Rosebery Street in reserve in case newer trams were destroyed in air raids. It was eventually broken up in June 1945 having never run again after the closure of the Dudley Road services at the end of this day. (R.T. Coxon)

Tram 97 stands at the end of the crossover in Soho Street just short of the 31 route terminus at Soho Railway Station. On the right is the hoarding carrying an advertisement for Parsley and Salmon Brand products which can be seen again in a fuller view on the opposite page. Behind the tram conductor is a group of late 1890s shops which stood on either side of Market Street. The conductor stands at the driver's end of the tram and is equipped with leather money satchel and bell-punch ticket machine. Presumably the ticket rack is somewhere on the tramcar. (Omnibus Society)

On Monday 23 September 1939, one week before the abandonment of the 31 service, UEC-bodied tramcar 75 stands outside the entrance to the LMS-owned Soho Station. Rabone Lane crosses at right angles at the distant junction. This tramcar was one of 150 four-wheelers which entered service between August 1906 and March 1907 with Mountain & Gibson Radial trucks. After a few years these trams suffered problems with the radial gear linkages and in the mid-1920s they were replaced with Brush Peckham trucks which gave a harsher ride but at least stayed on the track! Just visible above the railway bridge parapet is the White Horse public house. (J.S. Webb)

On 2 August 1938, the Radio Rodeo bill at the Birmingham Hippodrome shows Harold Ramsey and Buck and Chic who were the forthcoming attractions; Billy Scott-Coomber, also on the bill, was the main vocalist with the Jack Payne Dance Band. Facing back towards Birmingham, the crew of ex-Radial tramcar 125 pose alongside the entrance to Soho Station. (Birmingham Central Reference Library)

Safety helmets were not considered necessary when these workmen were widening the Soho Street Railway Bridge in 1965. Over the road is C. Walsh Graham's Timber Importer's yard while in the distance, the Windmill Lane flats are under construction. (Joe Russell)

Both the tram and the replacement bus routes terminated on the bridge above Soho Station, which was about three-quarters of a mile inside the Smethwick boundary. By the summer of 1968, the area around Soho Station had changed dramatically. The Bundy timekeeping clock had lost its mechanism, the B83 Birmingham-Soho via Heath Street route had recently lost its 'B' and Soho had lost its railway station nearly twenty years earlier. Even the Corporation buses were changing. Because of the closure of Rosebery Street garage on 29 June 1968, the 83 was operated from Quinton garage. No. 2552, (JOJ 552), was one of Quinton's Metro-Cammell-bodied Guy 'Arab' III Specials, whose chassis had been built to Birmingham's specification with a pre-selector gearbox and concealed 'New Look' radiator. No. 2552 entered service on 1 October 1950, surviving into WMPTE ownership until it was withdrawn on 28 February 1975. (L. Mason)

The White Horse public house, which appears in the 1861 census, is located at the junction with Rabone Lane, just beyond Soho Street railway bridge near to Soho Station's entrance. Mitchells & Butlers bought this pub in 1928 from Kingstone's Brewery Ltd of Great Arthur Street and planned to rebuild it in 1939 but this was never carried out. In the early 1960s, The White Horse had become a Banks's house and is still open today, renamed the Little Corner House. (M&B Crown Archive)

You can almost see Roberta from E.E. Nesbitt's *The Railway Children* standing on the embankment above the platform of Soho Station as they wait for their school's excursion sometime during the Edwardian period. The station was opened by the L & NWR on 1 April 1889 to cater for industrial workers and other passengers going to the nearby Cape Hill area. The station was between Monument Lane station, formerly known as Edgbaston and Smethwick and Rolfe Street. Gradually Soho Station fell victim to road transport competition and finally closed on 23 May 1949, just seventeen months into the British Railways era. (A. Maxam Collection)

The Soho Foundry Tavern at 154 Foundry Lane (formerly known as Sloe or Slough Lane). Mentioned as a beer house in a directory in 1856, it was conveniently situated opposite James Watt's Soho Foundry, built in 1796 (later becoming W.T. Avery), and was an ideal watering-hole for the thirsty foundry workers. It was rebuilt at the turn of the 1900s by Wood & Kendrick. In March 1961 a Ford car is parked outside the café owned by William Davies. (M&B Crown Archive)

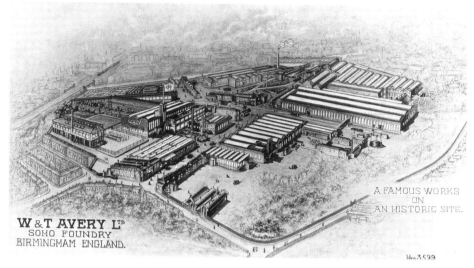

Soho Foundry Works was built by Matthew Boulton and James Watt in 1795-6 as the foundry for the Soho Manufactory and for years was the centre of steam-engine production. W&T Avery's acquired the historic works in 1895 for the production of weighing machines, ranging from small laboratory scales to weighbridges. Today the site is the headquarters of the American owned Avery Weigh-Tronix Group. (A. Maxam Collection)

The buildings on the right are late eighteenth-century workman's cottages in Foundry Row. These are historically important as on William Murdock's return to Soho from Cornwall in 1799, he lived in one of them. Murdock later moved into Sycamore Hill House, which was located just west of the nearby Queen's Head Road close to the main Soho Road in Handsworth. The remaining terraces in Foundry Row have survived as the sole reminder of either the Soho Manufactory or the Foundry. This row of restored eighteenth-century cottages survived although the end block was demolished to make way for the new post-war Avery gatehouse. (D.R. Harvey)

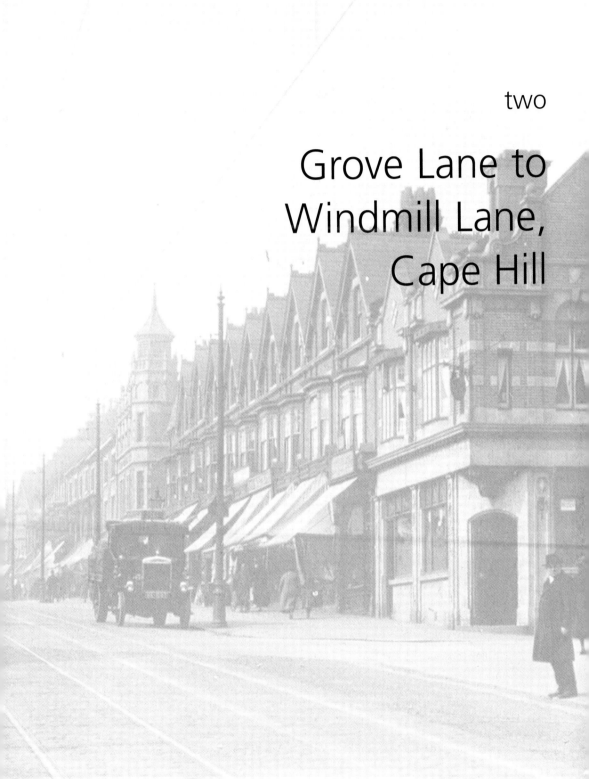

two

Grove Lane to Windmill Lane, Cape Hill

The Grove Cinema was located just inside the Birmingham boundary at 473 Dudley Road, the penultimate building in the city. The Grove Cinema was opened on 22 August 1932 with the film *Arsene Lupin* starring John and Lionel Barrymore. The B film showing at The Grove was a thriller entitled *Blondes For Danger*, starring the British actor Gordon Harker, (1885-1967) and directed by Herbert Wilcox. It finally closed on Saturday 24 October 1981. In 1938, tramcar 189 works on the Grove Lane 55 route short-working from Edmund Street to the nearby city boundary about 100 yards away outside the Cape of Good Hope public house.. Just prior to the expiry of the tram tracks' leases in Smethwick, Bearwood, Oldbury and Dudley, due on 30 September 1939, Birmingham Corporation offered to retain the 'main line' Dudley Road tram service 55 to the Grove Lane boundary. Included in this plan were the short Heath Street route to Soho (31), the Lodge Road service (32), and the 33 route to Ladywood. In the event the plan was rejected and only the 32 and 33 routes survived into the early post-war years. (Birmingham Central Reference Library)

Below: It is unusual for a public house to give its name to the surrounding area. This is the rear of the old, somewhat basic Cape of Good Hope building in 1901 when still a Mitchell's pub. Alongside it is the pub yard with a horse and covered dray about to set off on another delivery. The old pub was replaced by a much larger building designed by Wood & Kendrick which was reopened on 23 December 1925. This landmark pub was closed on 7 July 1994 and replaced by a McDonald's restaurant. (A. Maxam Collection)

The conductor of tramcar 124 has turned the trolley pole round and the tram is about to take the crossover onto the left-hand, inbound track before beginning the two-mile journey back on to the 55 service to Edmund Street terminus. The Smethwick, Bearwood, Oldbury and Dudley services continued up the distant Cape Hill, which rose from 465ft, just beyond the tram stop on the left, to 557ft at the Windmill Lane junction. Cape Hill was famous for having the Mitchells and Butlers brewery located on the left-hand side. It was set up by Henry Mitchell as the Crown Brewery in 1879. Less prestigious were the three-storied houses opposite the brewery which are visible beyond the tramcar. To the right of the tram is the Cape of Good Hope public house on the corner of Grove Lane. It is of some historical significance that everything to the west of Grove Lane might have been in Birmingham except for a vote taken by the Smethwick Board of Health in 1888 on a proposal that it should become part of its larger neighbour. The proposal was defeated by the chairman's casting vote! (Birmingham Central Reference Library)

In late July 1971, just prior to its withdrawal as the one of the last nine surviving Daimler CVD6s in WMPTE ownership that were allocated to Rosebery Street garage, 2768, (JOJ 768), stands in the miserable surroundings of Grove Lane near to the rear of the Grove Cinema and the front of the Cape of Good Hope. This bus had entered service at Rosebery Street garage on the 16 February 1952 and remained at that garage all its life. It stands at the terminus of the B80 route. The triangular sign to the right of the front of the bus marked the one end of the extent of the area in which the buses were allowed to park before leaving to go back to the city. (A. Yates)

Above left: Henry Mitchell's portrait, hung in the board room at Cape Hill Brewery. Mitchell (1837-1914) began to brew beer at the Old Crown, Oldbury Road, which he supplied to other pubs. As business thrived, Mitchell acquired a new, much larger site on the then open green fields at Cape Hill, where he moved in 1879. He formed Mitchells & Butlers with William Butler in 1897 and became its chairman from 1898 to 1914. Rapid expansion began – from a 14-acre site employing less than 300 people in 1900 to a 90-acre site employing over a 1,000 by 1914. He was a generous benefactor to the town and was made the first Freeman of the County Borough of Smethwick in 1902. One hundred years later, and by now owned by American brewers Coors, the Cape Hill brewery was closed. (A. Maxam Collection)

Above right: William Butler (1843-1907) was the licensee and brewer at the London Works Tavern in 1866 before moving to the Crown at Broad Street, Birmingham ten years later. His tower brewery at the back of the Crown survived until the 1980s when it was lost to the building of the ICC and Centenary Square. The Crown public house survives. (A. Maxam Collection)

Opposite above: When the Beehive pub at 153 Raglan Road, off Cape Hill, closed on 4 June 1968 for demolition, Mitchells & Butlers built a replacement also intended to be called the Beehive. The new pub, however, opened on 7 June 1971 as the Puffing Billy and was a typical example of 1960s architecture, blending in with the nearby Windmill Lane flats. A number of these early high-rise flats have been demolished. (M&B Crown Archive)

Opposite below: There are very few Victorian terraced houses left in Smethwick and even fewer of the rows of terraces with a common front entry. One of the victims of post-war redevelopment was Wills Terrace off Wills Street. In 1963, these solidly built houses dating from the 1870s, with two-storey tunnel-back terraces behind the end block of three storey houses, had only a few years left before being swept away by modern housing later in the 1960s. (Joe Russell)

The London Works Tavern at 35 London Street was at the junction with Grove Lane and appeared in a street directory of 1850. William Butler was the licensee and brewed on the premises in the 1860s and 1870s before he joined forces with Henry Mitchell. Little has changed externally since this picture was taken in 1964, though the interior has been modernised. (Joe Russell)

This aerial view shows the perimeter of the Cape Hill Brewery, 1920s. The large sports ground, with its County Championship standard cricket pitch, on which Worcester CC played an annual game, and the extensive railway sidings, feature prominently. (A. Maxam Collection)

Mitchells & Butlers maintained an impressive fleet of motor lorries for their deliveries. In 1929, at the Bottling Stores Deck in the Cape Hill Brewery yard, are over twenty lorries. Two are normal-control Leylands and include fleet numbers 51, (HA 1023) and 53, (HA 1025), the latter being the only vehicle present on pneumatic tyres. Most of the lorries under the loading bay, including number 8, which had a Birmingham rather than a Smethwick registration, dated from between 1919 and 1920, suggesting that these were renovated former War Department war surplus Army lorries. (A. Maxam Collection)

The voluntary Cape Hill Brewery Fire Brigade was founded in 1882 by Harry Mitchell, the co-founder Henry's son. The brigade quickly gained a reputation for its excellence and winning awards relating both to fire-fighting duties and sporting events. They were often called upon to assist local Municipal Brigades such as for the 1929 Theatre Royal fire. A new fire station was opened in 1927, nearer to the brewery gates, providing easier access to all areas of the brewery. This has survived the 2005 demolition. (A. Maxam Collection)

The distinctive original outer walls of Cape Hill Brewery were a local landmark. Even the illuminated Mitchells & Butler's 'Good Honest Beer' sign was partially lit up at night! In February 2005 the site was cleared to make way for the massive Mitchell's Brook housing estate, which at least recalls the name of the brewery founder. (Chris Ash)

Cape Hill is a very steep hill and here is a B&M tram (20) slowly grumbling its way past Durban Road in the 1920s. On the far side of Durban Road is the ornate late Victorian Smethwick Council Board School. On the extreme left is the local General Dispensary, built in 1888, which was the equivalent of a cottage hospital. It is noticeable that at this end of Cape Hill, away from the M&B Brewery, the quality of the houses was much better, being built in the 1880s with two-storied tunnel-back terraces with attics in the roof. Car 20 was built in 1904 by Brush and the batch was originally an open topper with a Lycett & Conaty 8ft 6in. radial truck. Trams of this type were supplied to all the BET Group of companies in the West Midlands, being collectively known as the 'Aston' type as they were first used in the Aston area. By this time the tram had been top-covered and fitted with a driver's windscreen. (D.R. Harvey)

While some areas of Smethwick have completely disappeared, other parts are still recognizably the same as they were eighty years earlier. On 14 August 2006, a Travel West Midlands Alexander-bodied Volvo B7TL, 4296, (BU 51 RYB), is seen here climbing up Cape Hill, albeit a little quicker than the tramcar over eighty years earlier. The General Dispensary building still looks imposing as it stands opposite the still thriving Cape Primary School at the entrance to Durban Road. Through the trees, to the left of the bus, a large number of the later Victorian houses have survived and been considerably modernised. On the right, the nineteenth-century Cape Hill shops are still trading. (D.R. Harvey)

The first purpose-built cinema in the town was the Cape Electric Cinema which opened in 1911 and closed in 1957. Located on the corner of Cape Hill and Rosebery Road, in 1925 the cinema was showing the film *Smouldering Fires*. This was a Universal Pictures drama starring Pauline Frederick and Malcolm McGregor. Travelling down Cape Hill is an ex-War Department Mitchells & Butlers Leyland brewery dray that had been registered in about 1920 with the mark HA 1090. The lorry is fitted with by then compulsory rubber tyres. It was not until 1925 that pneumatic tyres were allowed on vehicles over 3 tons in unladen weight. (A. Maxam Collection)

Once trams had hauled themselves up the steep Cape Hill as far as the Mitchells & Butlers Brewery (see the smoking chimney stack in the distance) the gradient lessened. This tramcar has about reached this point at the Salisbury Road junction, c. 1932. On the corner is the towered, Renaissance-style Barclays Bank which dated from 1907. To the left is a block dating from the 1890s, containing Woolworths and an England's shoe shop. Going down the hill is a strange-looking commercial traveller's two-seater car. Travelling to Oldbury on an 86 route working is BCT tram 195, which is being followed by a Model T Ford van. (D.R. Harvey)

A man walks past a footwear shop lighting a cigarette as the shop owner in a long apron looks on from his doorway, c. 1907. These properties were regarded as part of the best shopping centre to the west of Birmingham. On the south side of Cape Hill the late Victorian shops included, from left to right, Cadby's Drysalters, Simister's boot and shoe makers and George's Ironmongers, trading under the name of The Handy Stores. (A. Maxam Collection)

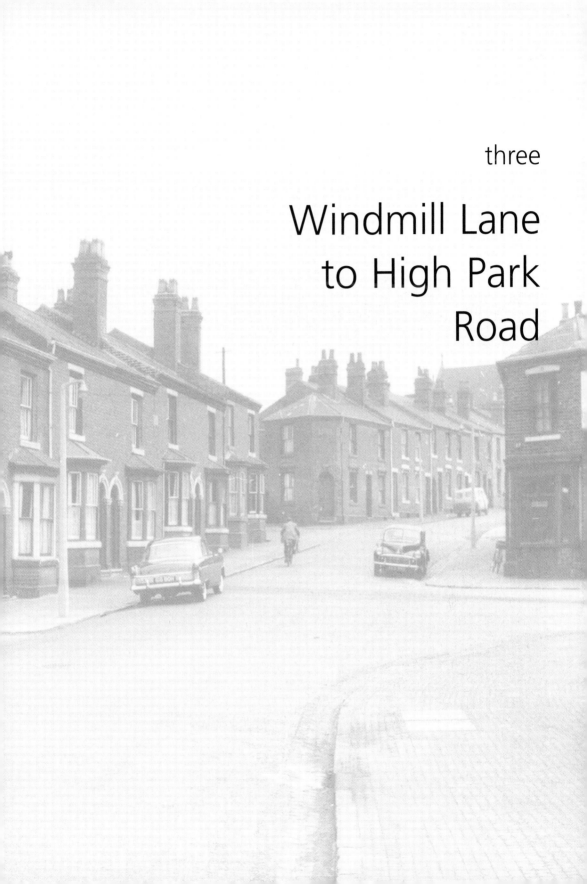

three

Windmill Lane to High Park Road

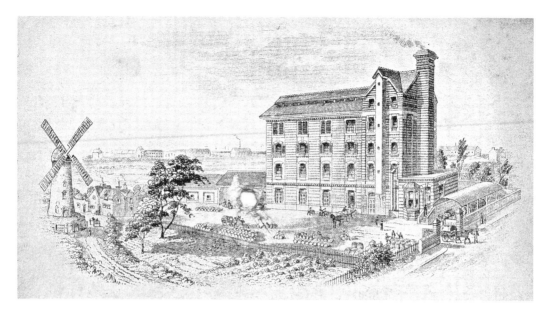

Cheshire's Windmill Brewery in Windmill Lane was registered as a partnership of Edward Cheshire and Benjamin Shakespeare in 1896. This drawing shows the brewery and the old windmill in about 1900 when still surrounded by fields. It was bought by Mitchells & Butlers in 1913. The nearby windmill, built by William Croxall in 1803, became part of the brewery eighty years later, and was only demolished in 1949. The old brewery was later used as a cold store by Scribbans who in a 1930s advertisement boasted that they were the 'largest cake makers in the world'. The building was demolished in 1960/1 and was replaced by flats. (A. Maxam Collection)

The Windmill Inn at 154 Windmill Lane occupied the corner with Ballot Street. The pub was listed in a street directory from 1855. The windmill, which later became part of the Cheshire's Brewery, used to stand across the road. The Windmill Inn has now closed, although the building still stands having been converted into housing. Behind the pub are numerous maisonettes and multi-storey flats which were built in the 1960s and had replaced the old Victorian housing. (M&B Crown Archive)

The church of St Matthew in Windmill Lane, given by J.W. Unett of the nearby Woodlands, was consecrated in 1855. Built of stone in the Decorated Gothic style it consists of a chancel, north vestry, aisled nave with north and south porches and the west bell tower with space for two bells; the architect was Joseph James. The vestry was added in 1892. In 1895 several memorials were erected in the church to Harry Mitchell. This is a part of Price Street which has since been shortened and at the Windmill Lane end has been built over with the Windmill Precinct. (A. Maxam Collection)

The vicarage of St Matthew's church was designed by Joseph James and built in Windmill Lane to the south-west of the church in 1856-7. It was given up in 1956 and demolished in 1958 and replaced by a new vicarage in 1969. (A. Maxam Collection)

Above: The redevelopment of the Windmill Lane area during 1965 demolished most of the Victorian housing but enabled the main A457 road to be widened. Looking south from the junction with Howard Street, St Matthew's church with its very narrow tower is on the left just beyond the Minivan which is travelling towards Cape Hill. (Joe Russell)

Left: The church of St Philip Neri in Messenger Road, (formerly High Park Road), was inaugurated by C.E. Ryder, a priest in Smethwick from 1882 to 1912. In 1904 he built the sacristies and the south transept containing this, the Lady Chapel. In 1908 the work was completed by adding the choir and the north transept containing the Sacred Heart Chapel. The church is a building of brick and terracotta designed by Alfred Pilkington of London. A marble high altar and sanctuary were installed as a memorial to Ryder in 1926. The church was finally consecrated in 1936. (A. Maxam Collection)

In about 1962 the corner of Poplar Street and Windmill Lane was dominated by R. George's long-established, large ironmonger's shop. Mr George's address even spanned two streets - 73 Poplar Street and 28 Windmill Lane. Outside the ironmonger's shop is a long-forgotten piece of street furniture – the fire brigade emergency telephone box. (Joe Russell)

The New Church Inn at 190 Windmill Lane was formerly a Cheshire's house and stood on the corner with Howard Street. Although this large mid-nineteenth-century building with its impressive wooden frontage and small leaded windows looks a picture of prosperity in 1963, it was subject to a compulsory purchase order and closed on 22 June 1969. Mitchells & Butlers moved the license to the new Hussar pub built in the nearby Windmill Precinct. (Sidney Darby)

Above: After the demolition of the Windmill Lane branch library the land was used as a parking lot. A 1965-registered Commer CA 7-ton lorry stands on the site. The Hussar public house was built here, replacing the New Church Inn seen in the distance to the left of the block of flats which overlooked Six Ways at the north end of Windmill Lane. (Joe Russell)

Below: By 1979, the redevelopment of the Windmill Lane area was complete with the loss of all the Victorian houses and shops which had occupied the area to the north of Cape Hill. Serving this redevelopment was new Hussar public house which opened with much ceremony on 19 October 1970. (Joe Russell)

At 1 High Park Road was the Victoria Hotel at the junction with Windmill Lane, Six Ways, which still looked prosperous in March 1961. The pub had first opened on 6 February 1892 and was closed in 1969. It had replaced the New Crystal Palace, which was not to be confused with the Old Crystal Palace which was in Cranford Street, Soho. (M&B Crown Archive)

The Red Lion public house at 33 Thomas Street on the corner with Baldwin Street was still trading in 1954. The hostelry was mentioned as early as 1845 when it was listed in a contemporary street directory. Despite considerable redevelopment in the area, the building still survives as housing. (M&B Crown Archive)

Messenger Road linked the Six Ways junction at Windmill Lane to a five-way junction near the railway bridge at Crocketts Lane over the Stour Valley main line between Birmingham and Wolverhampton. The Falcon Inn at the junction with Baldwin Street was looking like all the other buildings in the area in 1963, yet amazingly survived the wholesale demolition of the area and today with its surrounding 1970s housing area it is still thriving within yards of the Soho Way dual-carriageway. Watts Road is on the left while over the roof tops in Messenger Road part of the roof of St Phillip's Catholic church is just visible. (Joe Russell)

The Stork Inn at 17 Harding Street was situated at the junction with Brook Street and at this time, in 1950, Sidney Alan Swinden was the licensee. Formerly a Holder's Midland Brewery pub, the Stork Inn had a pair of well-etched windows and a splendid stone carving of a stork above the bar entrance. The pub fell victim to a compulsory redevelopment and closed on 31 March 1970. (M&B Crown Archive)

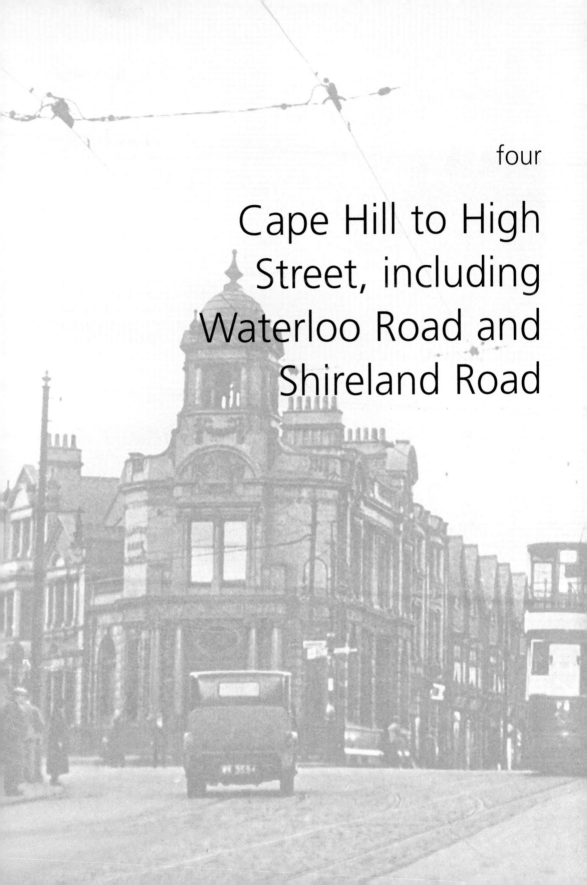

four

Cape Hill to High Street, including Waterloo Road and Shireland Road

The famous Birmingham-based Marsh and Baxter, who were renowned as one of the region's best pork butchers, had a large double-fronted shop at 26 and 28 Cape Hill in the block known as Five Ways Buildings. Looking from the first floor of the Lloyds Bank building, this view shows that Cape Hill was a thriving shopping centre. The shops extended towards Bearwood Hill to the left of the finger direction sign in the foreground, into Windmill Lane on the left and to the right, into both Shireland Road and Waterloo Road. Behind the ornate lamp-standard is the large Seven Stars Hotel. On the nearest corner of Windmill Lane is George Mason's grocery and provisions shop. With all these shops available, if any one said that they were 'going shopping up the Cape', they were going to a high quality suburban shopping centre. Passing into Cape Hill on its way to Dudley on an 87 working is tram car 136, near to the white-coated policeman on point duty.

BCT tram 72, the second of the 71-220 class, waits at the top of Cape Hill with Bearwood Hill behind it, just beyond the junction with Windmill Lane where Dewhurst's butchers shop is located on the left.

CAPE HILL, SMETHWICK.

It is about 1930 and car 72 is working on the 80 route, having come from St Paul's Road, Smethwick. The imposing Lloyds Bank on the apex of Bearwood Hill and Waterloo Road was built in about 1907 having replaced a large Georgian house called the Elms. On both sides of Bearwood Hill are rows of three-storied retail premises with a plethora of gabled attics.

Behind the trees is The Elms, a large eighteenth-century house which was demolished in 1906 to make way for the Lloyds Bank building. To the left is Waterloo Road where the retail premises rapidly gave way to houses. The Waterloo Stores on the corner of Shireland Road was a beer seller and later became the Waterloo public house. The two trams are working on the Windmill Lane service which had been introduced on 21 November 1904, three days before the service opened to Bearwood. The tram with 'Windmill Lane' showing on its destination box is B&M 22, a Brush-built 'Aston' type tram delivered in November 1904. The second tram is slowly negotiating the cross-over before moving onto the B&M tram stop. This open top, four-wheel tramcar has a three-figure fleet number showing it to be a City of Birmingham Tramways Company tram. Car 214 was built by CBT in late 1904 and it was on loan to the B&M in the spring of 1905 for about six weeks as the latter company was temporarily short of double-deck tramcars. 214 was a long-lived tram as it became BCT's 483 and was not withdrawn until March 1939, by which time it had been fitted with platform vestibules and an open-balconied top-cover.

The Waterloo Hotel at the Shireland Road junction with Cape Hill was originally to be called the Navigation and was built in 1907 on the site of Titus Mason's Waterloo Stores outdoor. Mason went on

to form Mason's soft drinks firm whose premises were in the nearby Grantham Road. The Waterloo Hotel was a Mitchells & Butlers showpiece public house and had been designed by the prolific pub architects Wood & Kendrick of West Bromwich. The interior featured superb tiled walls and ceilings. In June 1966 the impressive interior of the grill room had hardly changed since the pub had been built. (M&B Crown Archive)

On Thursday 6 January 1938, UEC ex-Radial class car 130 waits at the traffic lights in Waterloo Road with a 1935-registered Austin 10/4 saloon behind. The tram is about to cross in front of George Mason's shop on the corner of Windmill Lane which has the advertisement 'Cash Grocer' on its canvas awning. Above the horse and cart on the right is the Seven Stars Hotel while on the left is the 1907 stone-clad Lloyds Bank building. Car 130 was withdrawn in April 1939 after thirty-three years service. (Birmingham Central Reference Library)

A Mitchells & Butler's outdoor at 21 Waterloo Road on the corner with Gilbert Road was being run by Selina Wagstaff in March 1961. Next door and in the same Linden Place block is the newsagent and tobacconist owned by Frederick Akers. The double-fronted shop next door is that of British Relay Wireless Ltd. In Gilbert Road there was a row of unusual 1880s terraced houses which had three-storeys at the front, but only two storeys at the rear. Today the outdoor is now occupied by a taxi firm and the houses have been knocked down for a car park. (Sidney Darby)

A junior class of the Wesleyan Sunday school at Waterloo Road poses for the camera on 18 July 1914, a few weeks before the outbreak of the First World War. A mission was begun in the schoolroom at Shireland Hall in 1878 and had a membership of fourteen in 1880. They moved in 1886 to a new school chapel in Waterloo Road and this was replaced in 1896 by one on an adjoining site at the corner of Waterloo and Sycamore Roads. This chapel was designed by Ewen Harper in a brick-built Gothic style with stone dressings and a spired tower. It is now a Gurdwara Nanaksar Sikh Temple. (A. Maxam Collection)

In about 1910 Waterloo Road, in the vicinity of the Edgbaston Road junction, was a main road lined by a variety of styled late nineteenth-century houses. Unusually for a main road being used as a tram route, the overhead for both directions is mounted on single span arms. (A. Maxam Collection)

Left: In about 1898 the grocer's shop at the corner of Waterloo Road and Grange Road was run by Annie Maud Fowler, who stands in the doorway. Her husband Frank, with his hands in his waistcoat pockets, was a coal merchant. Later the shop became a newsagent's before being converted into private accommodation. (A. Maxam Collection)

Below: A Boy Scout band leads the procession up the steep hill in Shireland Road on a summer Sunday in July 1962. Processions, such as this one, stopped the traffic. A Hillman Minx Phase VII car is waiting for the band to pass. St Chad's church on the corner of Edith Road, was funded by Mitchells & Butlers. Built in 1900, the church replaced an iron mission building and survived until 1968. A petrol station now occupies this site. (Joe Russell)

In the early 1920s, ever-mindful of the opportunity of expansion, Mitchells & Butlers acquired five houses in Shireland Road as well as two at Montague Road on Smethwick's boundary with Edgbaston. They built the Shireland Inn which opened for trading on 17 April 1924. Some of the attractive stained glass used in this pub, made by Evans & Co of Oldbury Road, still survives above the bar. (M&B Crown Archive)

Beyond the crest of Cape Hill, towards Bearwood Hill, shops continued to Claremont Road. The tall, gabled Gospel Hall is on the right, and next to it, where the tram is standing, was the entrance to the Windmill Lane steam tram depot. On an Edwardian summer's day, about 1906, car 59, a B&M single-deck, closed combination monitor-style roof tram with a Lycett & Conaty 8ft 6in. radial truck, is working on the wrong line towards Smethwick because of the road works. These Kyotts Lake Road-built trams were made initially for the Rowley Regis route although they were later used on the Bromford and Spon Lane service. (J.H. Taylforth)

Bearwood Hill was absorbed into the High Street but originally stretched from Watery Lane to Windmill Lane. Looking towards Cape Hill in 1902, with Claremont Road off to the right, is the grand Market Place building, later occupied by the Co-operative Society, with the adjacent Gospel Hall built in 1901. Travelling towards Smethwick is a B&M Kitson steam tram locomotive pulling a double-deck trailer. The official plans to electrify the BMT main line were first published in September 1902 with double tracks from Grove Lane as far as Claremont Road. The steam tram route from Lionel Street in Birmingham ran as a five minute service starting at 5.30 a.m. and ending with an 11.21 p.m. departure. Better than today! (A. Maxam Collection)

The recently-opened Windmill Shopping Centre is intended to bring back shoppers to Cape Hill. The rows of Victorian shops were swept away along with the magnificent Gospel Hall building which moved to new premises in nearby Windmill Lane. The surviving nineteenth-century buildings are those on the corner of Claremont Road and those near to Windmill Lane. These date from the last few years of the 1890s and are characterised by some delicate Arts and Crafts-style wooden soffits. (A. Maxam)

West Smethwick Park was first laid out in 1889 and opened to the public some six years later as Victoria Park. It was built on the site of Pool Farm and at its entrance on Bearwood Hill was the impressive Lodge House. By 1908 Bearwood Hill was carrying the tracks of the B&M electric tramway which in good weather and on the occasion of special events would have brought many people to the park. The park was flooded during the heavy rainfall in July 1927. Since 2004 the Lodge House has housed the Smethwick Heritage Centre. (A. Maxam Collection)

Passing the entrance and Lodge of Victoria Park is car 88, one of the ubiquitous 71 class ex-Radial truck trams built in 1906. The park was opened to the public on 7 September 1895 after landscaping cost the amazing sum of £33,000, which was endowed by Sir James Chance, Bart. The 5-acre boating lake is supplied with water from a spring within the park which is one of the sources of the River Tame. Just inside the entrance is Smethwick's First World War memorial obelisk. Here on 12 April 1939 Birmingham City Transport's car 88 is travelling towards Dudley on the 87 service and has descended Bearwood Hill from the Windmill Lane and Cape Hill junction which is to the left of the tram. The tram is about to pass a 1936 Armstrong-Siddeley Standard 17 saloon car. (H.B. Priestley)

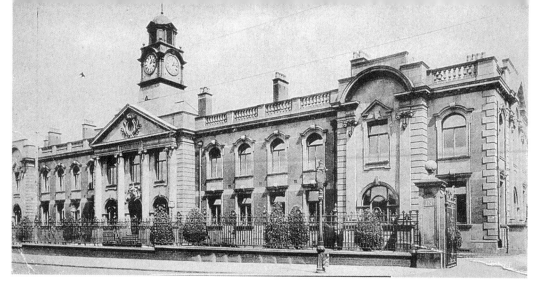

Smethwick Council House at the southern end of the High Street was built between 1905 and 1907 to the design of local architect Frederick J. Gill. The Council House is an impressive civic building set at the perimeter of Victoria Park behind its wrought-iron railings and was built by J. Dallow & Sons of Blackheath on a site adjacent Victoria Park, which had been formalised as public open space twelve years earlier. The Council House is made of Bath Stone and brick and is fashioned in a confused William and Mary period Baroque style with a central pediment and a clock tower which looks as though Mr Gill wasn't sure how to cap it off in a suitably imposing manner. (A. Maxam Collection)

Along this section of High Street, opposite the Council House in about 1908, the tramway traction poles have been given a fresh lick of paint. The ivy-covered house on the left stood on the junction with Watery Lane and, along with a line of other houses in the lane, was later demolished. Coopers Lane (now Firs Lane) is centre left behind the traction pole. Beyond that, opposite the tramcar, is the original Red Cow public house with its ground floor wooden facia. The tram is car 5, a double-deck open topper, and was one of the original B&M 1-12 trams built by Brush in 1904. These trams pre-dated the better known and slightly newer 'Aston' type tramcars. Victoria Avenue is a narrow passage beyond the Council House railings, above which is an advertisement on the gable for Collins Drug Store. (A. Maxam Collection)

Looking down from the High Street junction with Church Lane (today's Arden Road) towards the Council House and High Street in about 1910, some parcels of land were still not built upon. This lower section of Coopers Lane was renamed Firs Lane in the 1950s, after a large house which dated from the 1840s and stood on the corner Church Lane and Coopers Lane. The mid-nineteenth-century houses on the left have been largely rebuilt. The Firs Clinic medical centre was built on land on the right. (A. Maxam Collection)

The 'Great Smethwick Flood' occurred on 11 July 1927. Heavy rain had caused the water table to rise and water from the spring which sourced the boating lake in Victoria Park caused serious flooding. The boats from the same lake were used to ferry people to safety from a flooded area in High Street between John Street and Coopers Lane near to the Council House. Harrison's Fruit Stores was at 262 High Street and the shop still stands today occupied by a chemist. The posters on the railings referred to a forthcoming Bearwood Fair and this site was where the Red Cow was rebuilt in 1937. (A. Maxam Collection)

The original Red Cow was first mentioned in a deed of 1706 and was nearer to Coopers Lane than the new pub which was opened in 1937. The pub's sign was very unusual with a red cow standing on a grassy bank. In the road is a Bradford van and a 1951 West Bromwich-registered Fordson 5cwt, while on the pub's forecourt is a 1951 Standard Vanguard Phase 1. The row of shops with the unusual gabled attic in the roof was built at the end of the 1890s and contained a chemist, a florist, a confectioner, a hairdresser and an optician. Above the row of shops is the Baroque-style clock tower of Smethwick Council House.

An example of the stained glass of Thomas William Camm, whose studio was at 199 High Street at the corner of Regent Road, overlooking the old police station on the other side of High Street. Camm began working for Chance's Glass Works at the age of ten in 1849 and when Chance's ceased production of stained glass, Camm set up his own business in the heart of Smethwick. Members of the Camm's family carried the business on for some forty years after his death in 1912. The Camm Studio was demolished in the early 1980s.
(A. Maxam Collection)

Smethwick's original police station was built in 1860 and occupied a rather austere looking mid-Victorian double-fronted house in High Street, almost opposite Regent Street. Viewed in the early Edwardian period, this is 1905, two years before it moved to the current site in Piddock Street. (A. Maxam Collection)

Albert R. Rusgrove was primarily a shipping agent who transported goods rather than passengers. Next to the man on the right are advertisements for a positive roll call of international shipping lives such as Cunard, White Star and American Line. During the 1920s their booking offices were at 160 and 162 High Street. Rusgrove's shipping agency also sold pianos and organs as Mr Rusgrove was a part-time music teacher. (A. Maxam Collection)

Above: By 1962 Jagirder's International Food Stores at 181/183 High Street occupied the shop at the corner of Cross Street and was one of the first Asian-owned shops in the area. Parked outside the shop is a Morris J2 minibus. The houses next door in Cross Street with their multi-window panes suggest that these buildings are quite early Victorian properties for the Smethwick area. Most of Cross Street disappeared beneath Tollhouse Way. (Joe Russell)

Another part of the High Street area which was demolished in the development of Tollhouse Way was Union Street. At 135 High Street on the corner of Union Street was R.L. Morris's carpet and curtain shop. Mr Morris had moved into the premises in about 1958 having replaced the old established former ironmonger's business of Sidney Mason. (Joe Russell)

Right: The New Inn was at the eastern end of Union Street at the Crocketts Lane junction. The hostelry was listed in an 1845 street directory and this well maintained three-storey building looks as though it was this original structure, though by 1963 it had been strengthened by the addition of iron tie-bars. The pub was closed on 31 March 1971 and was demolished along with all the properties in Union Street soon afterwards to make way for Tollhouse Way. (M&B Crown Archive)

Opposite below: The Coronation of King George V took place on Friday 23 June 1911. All around the country street parties took place to celebrate the event and Union Street was no exception when the residents of the street proudly posed beneath the swathes of bunting with the street party in full flow. These houses dated from the 1840s and the whole street has now been swallowed up under the Tollhouse Way and Soho Way dual carriageways. (A. Maxam Collection)

In 1897, two shop assistants stand proudly for the camera at John Bragg's Model Bakery at 133 High Street. They had recently taken over the business of Hugh Smith who, according to the horse van parked in the street, was a pastry cook and confectioner. On the left is a large sign for Hovis Bread. This wholemeal bread had been developed in 1886 by a Staffordshire miller named Richard 'Stoney' Smith and it was named Hovis, abbreviated from *hominis vis* meaning 'strength of man'. At the Model Bakery entrance are the bakers with a grey horse harnessed up to a little delivery van. In the window of the bakery, the shelves are well loaded with cottage loafs and long batches while in the left-hand window are meat and pork pies. Over the provisions part of the shop on the right are some fifteen ham joints hanging on hooks; this was in the days before refrigeration and restrictive hygiene regulations.
(A. Maxam Collection)

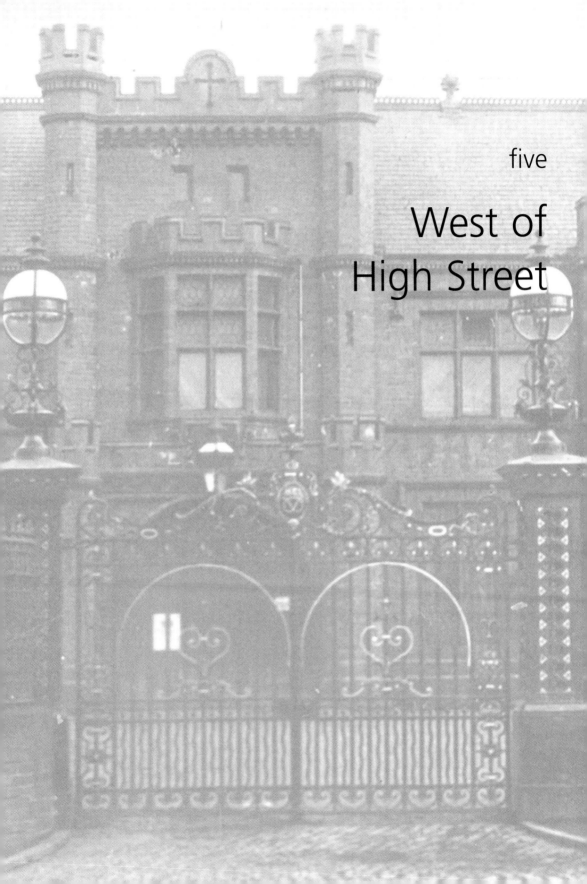

five

West of
High Street

Holy Trinity Schools, Trinity Street were at the junction with Church Hill Street. It was built as a National School for 400 children in 1840-1. More classrooms and a master's house were added in the 1860s, while further extensions were opened in September 1880 including an infants' department. In that year, after the building of the extensions, there were 224 boys, 210 girls, and 76 infants. The buildings were again extended and remodelled in the 1890s and soon gained a luxuriant growth of ivy. The schools were finally closed in 1939 and were destroyed by enemy action in 1940. The site is now occupied by Smethwick post office. (A. Maxam Collection)

Left: Holy Trinity church in Trinity Street was built in 1837 and consecrated in 1838 to serve the growing population of north Smethwick. Holy Trinity became the parish church for the newly created parish of North Harborne in 1842. The original church, designed by Thomas Johnson of Lichfield, was enlarged in 1887-89 to designs by Francis Bacon of Newbury, although the original tower and spire were retained. (A. Maxam Collection)

Opposite above: Extensive bomb damage occurred in the Church Hill Street area on the night of 12 December 1940. This was the sixth air raid on Smethwick. Looking downhill towards Stony Lane, on the right is William Fox & Sons, Mechanical Engineers, whose premises were extensively damaged, although they were later rebuilt. A parachute mine landed in moulding sand at Samuel Smith's Beehive Foundry at Brewery Street and left an enormous crater as well as destroying the entire foundry and surrounding buildings. (South Staffs Water)

Below: In about 1925, the tree-lined South Road looking from High Street end was one of the better addresses in Smethwick with large semi-detached villas lining either side. The pillar box on the left side of the road is near the crossroads with Green Street. The Smethwick ex-Servicemen's Club now stands on the right. (A. Maxam Collection)

After Mitchells & Butlers had rebuilt the Hollybush at The Uplands in 1903, they wanted to upgrade it from a beerhouse to a full licensed house. It was now a public house in everything but name, being described as 'a large and commodious house, occupying a very desirable position… near the Drill Hall, tennis courts, cricket, football and hockey grounds… whose members wished to be supplied with spirits…' in the *Birmingham Post* in 1906. (M&B Crown Archive)

The Drill Hall at Broomfield was near the junction with The Uplands. It was presented by Henry Mitchell, founder of the Mitchells & Butlers brewery, who gave fourteen acres of his land to the Borough of Smethwick in 1894 in memory of his son, Harry, who died of typhoid fever aged thirty-two. By the Edwardian era, the Drill Hall had become the Territorial Army headquarters of the Royal Engineers division. It became the Harry Mitchell Recreation Centre in the late 1960s. (A. Maxam Collection)

The Harry Mitchell Park, north of Parkes Street, was laid out on six of the fourteen acres of the land which Henry Mitchell gave to the town in 1894. As though to encourage healthiness, incorporated into the park was a children's gymnasium, pictured here around 1905, with its swings, benches, see-saws and climbing frames. The park also had a cricket ground and a bandstand at the centre of a formal garden. (A. Maxam Collection)

Smethwick Hall was a large two-storied Georgian house built in 1746 with a porticoed entrance at the centre of a five-windowed frontage. The hall was demolished in 1937 after most of the land had been disposed of for suburban development. Part of the remaining open land was retained and laid out as a park centred on a small pool. The latter had been used as a reservoir for the nearby Birmingham Canal and is now known as Smethwick Hall Pool. In about 1918, Londonderry Lane leads up to the drive and Lodge at the junction with Stony Lane. (A. Maxam Collection)

Hall Road, in the Uplands area of Smethwick is named after Smethwick Hall. With its early 1930s semi-detached houses, Hall Road runs between Londonderry Lane to the north into the heart of the 1930s estate at Greenfield Road, which in turn gets its name after Greenfield House. (A. Maxam Collection)

This bus, a 1939 SOS FEDD with a Brush H30/26F body, BMMO 2352, (FHA 856), is waiting near to the Atkinson's Brewery's Londonderry public house, in Warley. The open bonnet suggests something serious has happened and the crew are wondering what to do next with their ailing charge. Warley was still largely rural until the late 1920s when large housing estates were built in the area to the northwest of Bearwood and south of Smethwick. The area was completely suburbanised with municipal housing by the late 1930s and this was quickly exploited by the Midland Red company. (A.B. Cross)

six

Rolfe Street

Above: A former Midland Railway 2F 0-6-0 locomotive at the head of a local train to Wolverhampton High Level Station drifts into Smethwick Rolfe Street Station on 30 May 1959. Rolfe Street was one of the original seven intermediate stations on the L&NWR's Stour Valley line which opened on 1 July 1852. Because the station was on a curve, it had staggered platforms with the waiting rooms and entrances to both up and down platforms at the bottom of the steps from the street-level booking hall. To accommodate the long passenger trains to and from Birmingham or Wolverhampton, the platforms at the Birmingham end of the station seemed to stretch halfway to Soho Station! (MilePost 92½)

Opposite below: The Station Inn, formerly a Cheshire's house, stood at 1 Rolfe Street at the junction with North Western Road, over the road from Rolfe Street railway station and a few doors away from the Theatre Royal. It was a typically imposing late Victorian hostelry built specifically to catch the nineteenth-century commuters, but was to close in 1970 and the site is now occupied by a clothes factory. (M&B Crown Archive)

Right: A souvenir programme from the 1920s shows the frontage of the Theatre Royal in Rolfe Street. Opened in 1897, it was one of the largest and most successful provincial theatres in England with a capacity of nearly 3,000. It closed in 1932 when the proprietors went bankrupt and was sometimes used to stage boxing matches until demolition in 1940. A serious fire at the residential flats next door resulted in eleven people losing their lives in 1929. (A. Maxam Collection)

Below: Until 1837 the inhabitants of Smethwick had to go to Birmingham to send and collect mail. In 1890 a new head post office was opened in Rolfe Street. It was replaced by the office in Trinity Street in 1968, though the original building still stands. The occasion for this posed group outside the post office is not recorded. (Norfolk, Lamprey and John/A. Maxam Collection)

It is Saturday 3 August 1957 and a 4-6-0 5XP 'Jubilee' class locomotive is about to go underneath Rolfe Street bridge before passing non-stop through the station on its way to Birmingham New Street. On the left is the old goods station whose northern end was dominated by Sam Price's potato merchant's warehouse, which backed on to the premises on the north side of High Street. To the right are the blue brick walls which lined both sides of the strangely shaped North Western Road. The walls separated this road from, on this side, the railway line, and on the far side from the 453ft level of the 1828 'New Cut' which was designed by Thomas Telford for the Birmingham Canal Navigations. In the trees on the right is the Smethwick New Pumping Engine which was built in 1892 and housed two compound steam engines which lifted water from the new Telford canal some 20ft to the 1773 Brindley canal. (D.J. Norton)

The Boatman public house was at 31 Great Arthur Street, which was originally a dead-end street running off Brasshouse Lane and was later extended to Roebuck Lane. It backed on to Brindley's Wolverhampton Level of the Birmingham Canal from which it got its name. There is snow on the ground during the freezing winter of 1963. The pub was mentioned as The Boat in an 1834 directory and appears in the 1851 census as The Boatman's Inn. Acquired by M&B in 1940, it closed for trading on 3 January 1971 and was replaced by low-rise housing. (M&B Crown Archive)

Above: The District Iron and Steel Works was founded in 1867 alongside the Birmingham Canal on the site of Smethwick Brass House foundry which was Smethwick's first known industrial site. They made steel tubes for bedsteads, telephone poles, aerial masts, car exhaust pipes, corrugated fencing and railway sleepers, while later they went into galvanising and cadmium plating. The District Iron and Steel Works continued until closure in 1985. New roads and housing have now encroached onto the site whose entrance had been in Brasshouse Lane. (A. Maxam Collection)

Below: Occupying a dominant position at the junction of Lewisham Road and Downing Street, the Old Navigation Inn faces Bridge Street which crosses the Stour Valley Railway main line and the two branches of the Birmingham Canal to the north. It appears in the census of 1851, along with the New Navigation Inn which stood near the canal at nearby Bridge Street. This is 27 July 1950, when George Arm, the landlord, had already run the pub for over twenty years. (M&B Crown Archive)

The late Victorian Waggon & Horses was at the corner of 84 Lewisham Road and Cambridge Road and was granted a full license in 1925. The pub had superb windows with the legend 'Waggon & Horses' etched on them. At the top of the building to the upper right is a relief of the name carved in stone. (M&B Crown Archive)

The British Engineer was at 179 Wellington Street. By March 1961, this back street Victorian pub had originally been owned by Holder's Midland Brewery of Birmingham until they were taken over by M&B in 1919. It stood for at least a century before closing on 16 May 1965 for demolition. (Sidney Darby)

The Crown and Anchor Inn at 65 Cross Street was at the junction of Rolfe Street and was listed in a street directory of 1855. It was formerly a Henry Mitchell pub before the formation of Mitchells & Butlers. Seen here in March 1961, a Bedford S-type lorry travels along Rolfe Street and the Crown and Anchor still looks well-looked after. All the surrounding houses have now been cleared and the pub closed for trading on 7 September 1975. (Sidney Darby)

The grandly named Star & Commercial Hotel was at 151 Rolfe Street on the junction with Bridge Street and was listed in a street directory of 1855. By March 1961 it was known just as the Star Inn and it closed in 1997, though the building still currently stands. Beyond the Austin A40 Farina, a Standard Vanguard III, a Ford Anglia E93A and a Ford Prefect E493A are parked outside an old three-storey terrace whose crumbling gable end has had to be supported by huge wooden props. (Sidney Darby)

The Staffordshire Knot public house was on the corner of Rolfe Street and Rabone Lane with the public bar overlooking the junction. Formerly a Cheshire's house, this building replaced an earlier pub and was built in 1892. The pub closed in 1980 although the building still stands. (M&B Crown Archive)

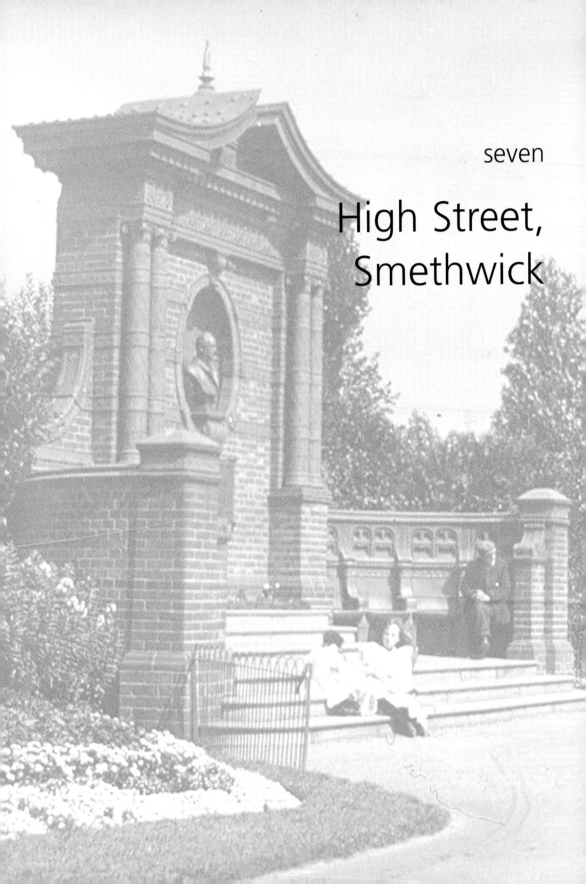

seven

High Street, Smethwick

Above: Beyond the Congregational church's railings in this view from around 1929, Mrs A. Perrin's drapery shop is on the extreme left at 128 High Street while next door the Smethwick sub-post office was run for many years by Miss Fanny Elizabeth Blomer. Beyond the next three shops occupied by a tailor, a greengrocer and, somewhat curiously, the Rowley Regis Granite Quarries Company, is the impressive Midland Bank Building on the corner of Brewery Street. Travelling towards Birmingham on an 86 service is tramcar 118, one of the ex-Radial truck cars built by UEC in 1907. (A. Maxam Collection)

This artist's impression of the new Lloyds Bank building came from a contemporary edition of the *Smethwick News Telephone*. The newspaper stated that there were few architectural buildings of note in Smethwick; (a similar comment was made by the architectural historian Nikolaus Pevsner in 1968). This was at least partly remedied in 1906 by the building of the Council House and this 'splendid addition' at the corner of High Street and Brewery Street. Lloyds Bank wanted a new prestigious branch. This Renaissance-style building featured red Lilleshall bricks, grey terracotta and a copper cupola roof with suites of offices on the first floor. (Smethwick Library)

Opposite below: The corner of Rolfe Street and High Street, occupied by George Newbury's linen drapery shop which started trading there in about 1870 and lasted until 1932. The shop was taken over by Samuel Smith who manufactured 'Firesight' grates in nearby Brewery Street although the corner continued to be known as Newbury's Corner. The shop was bombed in December 1940. Also fondly remembered by Smethwick folk is Welch's Department store, established since 1849. They built a single-storey building in 1962 as an extension to their existing three-storied premises at 123-127 High Street. (Joe Russell)

Before the First World War, this view eastwards towards Crocketts Lane and the Council House along High Street shows that the small early Victorian domestic style of shops had given way with the much larger, more confident-looking buildings. Children are gathered outside the London City and Midland Bank, with its distinctive dome, and Lloyds Bank is on the opposite corner of Brewery Street. On the left is the Rolfe Street junction with Newbury's linen drapery store. The distinctive triangle-topped building in the distance was James Parson's house furnishing shop. (A. Maxam Collection)

By 2005, here, the banks, now HSBC and Lloyds TSB, are still operating though the row of buildings stretching from Rolfe Street to Regent Street have gone. The former Congregational church was bought by Sikhs in 1961 and converted, with the addition of an ornate dome, into the Guru Nanak Gurdwara temple. Now totally reconstructed, this was the first Gurdwara in Europe and has ten rooms, including a school, library, sports hall and offices. (A. Maxam)

OLD TOLL HOUSE BLUE GATES.

A steamroller is about to turn into Stony Lane from Smethwick's High Street here in about 1910 while people standing outside the toll house watch the trundling vehicle. On the other side of Brasshouse Lane, opposite the toll house, is the George Inn, at this time selling Rushton's Ales. To the right of the goods station the posters on the hoardings for the L&NWR advertise such journeys as Manchester for 3s 3d and excursions to London for 5s. (A. Maxam Collection)

While the buildings on the Smethwick Library side of the street have thriving businesses, those on the side adjacent to the railway main line do not exist any more. With the exception of the toll house and the former goods station, all have been replaced by Tollhouse Way. The original toll house had been built on the corner of High Street and Brasshouse Lane in 1767 and was replaced in 1818 by the present Regency-styled building. The neat, almost church-like windows are in a quite ordinary square-shaped house, except that there is a triangular extension which is where the toll-office was located. The three round-topped windows on the ground floor gave an all round view along the High Street and enabled the toll-master to observe approaching travellers. Even in the 1820s, the amount of goods being carried by road through Smethwick was considerable and had to pass the toll house, which made a considerable profit for nearly the next fifty years. (A. Maxam)

Above: The police look on, with the George Inn behind them, as the workmen remove a section of the old pedestrian bridge and steps in 1966. This bridge joined High Street and Brasshouse Lane. As well as using a mobile crane, the contractors are using a one-year old Ford D-Series articulated lorry and an older Bedford S-type tractor unit. (Joe Russell)

Below: The demolition of the north side of the High Street was almost complete by 1981 in preparation for the construction of Tollhouse Way. This made the A457 Dudley Road into the Smethwick dual carriageway bypass running from the Grove Lane boundary to Oldbury. Most of the buildings by this stage had been knocked down apart from the George Inn, at the junction with Brasshouse Lane, which had closed on 22 February of that year and was still awaiting its fate. (Joe Russell)

Well-dressed children pose for the camera in the middle of the High Street in about 1908. On the left is the toll house and beyond it is the George Inn. The more important buildings in Smethwick were built in High Street with perhaps the best known being the original nineteenth-century Town Hall and the library which were built directly opposite the toll house. Next to this civic building on the corner of Stony Lane, on the extreme right, is the second Blue Gates Hotel which was built in about 1850 and which was replaced by the present hotel in 1932. This Blue Gates public house had a large lantern street light above its entrance, just visible above the young boy and girl standing on the kerb outside the library. (A. Maxam Collection)

Smethwick's Public Hall in High Street was designed in a Gothic style by the well-known Birmingham architect Yeoville Thomason in 1867, who also designed Birmingham's impressive Council House. The Smethwick Council House became the library in 1927/8 having been rendered largely redundant as a public building after the new, larger Council House had been opened in 1907. Here in 1963 it still retained its original front entrance prior to removal to the side of the building next to the Blue Gates Inn on the right. (Joe Russell)

Above: A decorated Blue Gates, High Street shows the staff posing for the camera, for the Coronation of George V in June 1911. First mentioned as a pub in a document from 1781, the pub got its name from the toll gates through which pedestrians, mounted horses and waggons had to pass as they travelled along the turnpike road between Birmingham and Dudley. The current larger public house was opened 7 October 1932. (A. Maxam Collection)

Looking west from the junction with Stony Lane towards West Smethwick in about 1914 showing a thriving and bustling shopping centre. On the left is Nelson's butchers shop with the shop assistant standing outside the shop wearing a slightly blood-stained apron. Beneath the row of five hanging lamps is one of the ubiquitous James Dallaway's greengrocer's shops. (A. Maxam Collection)

Above: The same view on Christmas Day 2005 shows that the line of shops on the left is still recognisable but the demolition of shops on the other side has left a rather uneven look to High Street. (A. Maxam Collection)

Opposite below: The North Western Inn at 80 High Street at the junction with Ford Street was little more than a rather well-proportioned mid-Victorian double-bay windowed house with a central porch entrance. The North Western was recorded in the 1871 census and closed as a pub on 31 March 1970, reopening three years later as a private club called the Red Fort which is still trading. (M&B Crown Archive)

A distant Oldbury-bound tramcar negotiates the numerous horse-drawn waggons as it passes Halford Street in about 1914. On the right is the impressive Edwardian terrace of gabled-roofed shops with Dibble Road at the end of the block. The shops were occupied by companies such as the provision dealer Maypole Dairies. A horse and delivery cart for E. Campbell is parked outside this row of shops. On the left is the three-storied Crown Inn with its distinctive name board. (A. Maxam Collection)

The same view in 2005 looking towards Dibble Street shows how the area on the left has been cleared, adjacent to Tollhouse Way. On the right, the high quality Edwardian shops have been given a general 'makeover' and are still very much in business. (Andrew Maxam)

Alterations to the shop frontages in High Street were the order of the day in 1962 although nineteen years later the row was to be demolished. J.R. Broadway Butcher's shop was about to open up at Nos 65 and 67, having taken over the business from Frank Bridges. Miss A.C. Halford's Wool Shop was next door at No. 69 and gave Green Shield Stamps with purchases of Paton and Baldwin's wool. (Joe Russell)

The licensee, possibly George Price Davies, wearing his barman's apron, stands purposefully outside the Crown Inn at 47 High Street in about 1907. The pub's greatest claim to fame was that it had been run by Henry Mitchell in the 1860s before he joined forces with William Butler to brew beer. The Crown public house closed for trading on 22 February 1981, prior to this side of the High Street being demolished for the Tollhouse Way scheme. (A. Maxam Collection)

The Empire Theatre was in St Paul's Road and was built in 1910 to the design by George Bowden & Son of Smethwick. It was intended for use both as a theatre and as a cinema but between 1930 until its closure in 1957 the Empire was used solely as a cinema, although in 1961 the building still looked like a cinema. In 1971 the building was converted into shops and it is now a centre for Asian Education. On the left is St Paul's Road, while to the right of the little triangular piece of tree-lined greenery is the Oldbury Road. This junction was the terminus for the rarely operated B84 bus service. (Joe Russell)

Opposite above: Car 7, a B&M tram, waits in Oldbury Road at the St Paul's Road short-working terminus in about 1906. The tram is standing just beyond the end of the High Street and is outside a mixed row of early and mid-nineteenth-century cottages though there is a pair of larger bay-windowed houses to the right of the distant tram standard. Two young girls in smocks pose in front of a pair of Georgian, porticoed cottages while alongside car 7 is the driver and conductor. The tramcar was one of twelve, (1-12), built by Brush in 1904 which were fitted with Brush 'AA' 6ft 6in. wheelbase trucks and a Bellamy-style top cover which had sliding roof panels and no canopy over the balcony. The name Bellamy is that of the Liverpool Corporation's General Manager, who introduced the design. (D.R. Harvey)

Opposite below: Fenton Street runs slightly downhill from St Paul's Road and Oldbury Road, where, in this view from around 1964, the distant hoarding has the iconic advertisement 'Drinka Pinta Milka Day'. On both sides of the road were rows of Victorian tunnel-back houses. On the left at the St Paul's Road corner was the Smethwick Motor Garage. Alongside the garage is a Ford Thames 305E 5cwt van which is parked in front of an Austin A40 Farina, while parked opposite, next to the concrete garages, is a 1955 Standard 8. (Joe Russell)

Above: On the corner of Devonshire Road and St Alban's Road was St Alban the Martyr church. This was consecrated in 1906, becoming the parish church three years later. The church is of red brick with stone dressings and was designed in a vaguely Tudor style by F.T. Beck of Wolverhampton with a clerestoried nave, two aisles, an apse, but strangely only a bellcote tower over the West door. A vestry was added in 1958. (A. Maxam Collection)

Below: Members of the Ebenezer Cricket Club pose for the camera in the summer of 1913. The team played in the Second Division of the Smethwick and District League, though for this photograph they appear to only have ten players. (A. Maxam Collection)

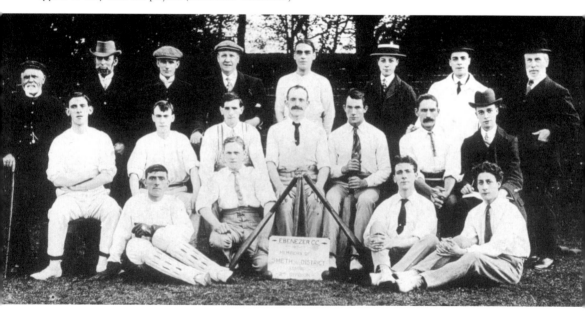

Above left: An engraving of St Paul's church, St Paul's Road, Smethwick that appeared in the *Illustrated London News* on 16 October 1858. The church was designed in the Early English style by G.B. Nichols of West Bromwich with a tall, steeply pitched roof over the nave, a north transept and a tall spire on top of the tower. Further expansion occurred in 1920 when a chapel and a south transept were added. Unfortunately, the nave of this large church was destroyed by fire on 3 February 1963. (A. Maxam Collection)

Above right: A replacement fibreglass spire was added to the original tower of St Paul's church in 1961 because of severe structural problems with the 1858 steeple. The church was destroyed by fire two years later, but was rebuilt by 1966 with the old tower and part of the north wall being incorporated into the new design. The spire is now an exhibit at the Avoncroft Museum, Bromsgrove. (Joe Russell)

The charred remains of the interior of St Paul's church after the fire of February 1963 destroyed the nave, although most of the organ loft, pipes and the instrument seemed to have survived. A new contemporary-styled church was built over the east end of the former building, which was designed by Denys Hinton & Associates incorporating the original church tower. (Joe Russell)

The 51¼-acre West Smethwick Park was given to the town by Sir James Timmins Chance (1814-1902) and was opened by him on 7 September 1895 on land previously farmed by the Downing family. The park contained two lodges, a refreshment room and a boathouse as well as a 5-acre boating lake, the Chance Memorial and one of the park lodges. Chance was made a baronet in 1900 and was associated with the development of lighthouse glass at his Spon Lane Works. He was also prominent in local and county affairs and became High Sheriff of Staffordshire in 1868. (A. Maxam Collection)

This coach, named Desert Cloud, was an Albion Victor PJ 26 and is parked for a publicity photograph outside the Lodge at West Smethwick Park in about 1932. The coach had the fleet name Eddystone Coaches, which was a wordplay on Edward Stone who was the proprietor. W.E Stone was based in Bertram Road, which was between St Paul's Road and Devonshire Road. (A. Maxam Collection)

eight

Oldbury Road

Above: One of Smethwick's older pubs was the Swan Inn on the corner of Oldbury Road and Holly Lane. It was first listed in 1834 as a home-brew pub. This building replaced the earlier one in 1933. It was formerly owned by Aston-based Atkinson's Brewery. Although Atkinson's was taken over by Mitchells & Butlers in 1959, the Swan Inn was still carrying its Atkinson sign in March 1961. After 160 years of trading, it was demolished in 2003 after being the subject of an arson attack. (Sidney Darby)

After thirty years of congestion, canal directors decided that drastic measures were needed to improve the fifty year-old James Brindley, Wolverhampton Level waterway. In 1824 Thomas Telford had referred to it as 'little better than a crooked ditch' and his suggestion was to lower it by 20ft ('the Birmingham Level'), enabling the canal to take a straight line from Birmingham to Smethwick and removing all intervening locks. The 'new line' opened on 18 December 1829 and at its deepest point Telford built one of Britain's great bridges, Galton Bridge, named after Samuel Galton, a banker on the Navigation Committee. The bridge carries Roebuck Lane majestically over it with an arch span of 154ft. In 1829 this was one of the largest iron bridges in the world. It was made by the Horseley Iron Works, who built many of the iron bridges over Black Country canals. Looking here towards Oldbury from tow-path level, the magnificent Grade I listed structure is seen in all its glory. A horse pulls a loaded narrow boat towards Smethwick as a bargee sits on the stern and on the other side of the canal, on the extreme left, is the arch over the Stour Valley railway opened in 1852. Through Galton Bridge is the three-arched brick bridge carrying the GWR's Stourbridge Extension railway which opened in 1867. (A. Maxam Collection)

Opposite below: Tram 89 trundles back towards Smethwick and Birmingham at the Roebuck Lane junction. The UEC-bodied four-wheel tramcar is negotiating the unusual interlaced track in Oldbury Road when working on the 85 service from Spon Lane on 30 September 1939 – the last day of operation on 'The Track'. The use of white paint on street furniture and kerbing indicates that war-time blackout conditions were in place. In the background, the Vauxhall car is about to turn into Roebuck Lane and travel over Thomas Telford's magnificent Galton Bridge, constructed in 1828 above the Birmingham Level of the Birmingham Canal and the Stour Valley railway line. (L.W. Perkins)

On the short section of two-line working between Galton Junction, behind the large bushes on the right, and the railway bridge in Roebuck Lane, there was a landslip following torrential rain on 11 July 1927. The steep-sided embankment collapsed and much of the mud flow went into the Birmingham Canal, filling it for about 60 yards. The infilled section must have dried out quite quickly as a large number of people are seen here standing on it having gained access to the tow path from Roebuck Lane. Repair gangs are in the area around Galton Junction, emptying the long line of wagons that have arrived with spoil to stabilize and rebuild the landslip. In the distance is Galton Junction signal box. (A. Maxam Collection)

Opposite above: The arrival of a train is imminent at Galton Junction on 15 June 1957. Looking towards Wolverhampton, Galton Bridge signal box is on the right of the tracks while beyond that is Roebuck Lane Railway Bridge with Galton Bridge its continuation over the canal on the extreme right. Galton Junction was opened on 1 April 1867 as a link between the L&NWR Stour Valley main line between Birmingham and Wolverhampton and the GWR's Stourbridge Extension line. Beyond the, just visible, second bridge on the main line is the location of the present day Galton Bridge Station with its high level platforms on the bridge which carries the line to Stourbridge. This new station, with its complex of lifts linking the low-level main line to the high level branch line, was opened on 24 September 1995. (D.J. Norton)

Opposite below: Summit Bridge in Roebuck Lane, built in 1789, was a typical eighteenth-century carting bridge over Brindley's original Birmingham Canal. By the 1960s, the bridge was becoming far too narrow for the ever-increasing amount of traffic. A Midland Red D7 double-decker, 4368, (VHA 368), is working on the 252 route which ran a 15-minute service between Cape Hill and Carter's Green by way of High Street, Smethwick, Roebuck Lane and High Street, West Bromwich. This bus was briefly fitted with an experimental semi-automatic gearbox but by this time, in 1963, the driver was struggling with the old 'stick and clutch' method. (A.D. Broughall)

Facing Smethwick, Oldbury Road had a small row of shops around Nine Leasowes. In 1965, before major redevelopment took place, the original Waggon & Horses public house on the right was at the junction with Nine Leasowes. The row of late Victorian shops on the right included Wilson's butchers shop while next to it was Arter's newsagents, tobacconists and drapery business. (Joe Russell)

The Oldbury Road in 1979 shows road widening and construction of the Sandfield and Malthouse high-rise blocks. The Le Corbusier concept of 'Cities in the Sky' would not last long in Smethwick as the flats were demolished at the end of the 1990s. The old Waggon & Horses closed in 1966 for demolition, although the block of shops on the right survived intact and unchanged during this period. (Joe Russell)

The new Waggon & Horses was opened in 1970 and was set back from the road, but lacked the style of the original building. In the early 1990s it was renamed Desi2. A truncated Nine Leasowes leads up the hill beyond the disappearing Volkswagen Beetle saloon to the distant St Paul's Road. Next to the pedestrianised section of Nine Leasowes in the foreground is Wilson's butchers shop. (Joe Russell)

The Ruskin Pottery Works, with its distinctive chimney behind the factory, stood at 173 and 174 Oldbury Road. The Ruskin earthenware manufactory was founded by Edward Richard Taylor in 1898 and was managed by his son William Howson Taylor until 1935 when the factory closed. With no one to take over the company, he took the secrets of the brightly coloured glazes to his grave. The house on the left, seen here in about 1922, was occupied by Doctors Smout and Brown. (Joe Russell)

The strangely shaped, 1920s-built Barclays Bank at the junction with Mallin Street is seen here in a photograph from 1964. Redevelopment later destroyed this once thriving area. A Ford Zodiac II 206E model is parked outside Fred Harding's gentlemen's hairdressers' saloon. Around Oldbury Road's junction with Mallin Street are groups of railings to protect pedestrians at this road junction, which still displays the black and white wartime black-out markings. (Joe Russell)

Oldbury Road on the west side of Mallin Street, opposite Spon Lane, had a shopping row continuing for another ten retail outlets, seen here in 1964. The first one next to the Mallin Street junction, with the police box on the corner, is the sub-post office and next door is G. Phillip's 'sweetie shop'. (Joe Russell)

In the 1960s, shops on the Oldbury side of Mallin Street in Oldbury Road included R.S. Paskin's ironmongers and electrical store in a post-war re-fronted building. They were advertising Black & Decker and Wolf Drills and sold Esso Blue paraffin, famous for the 'Esso Blea Dooler' adverts on television. In the gap between Paskin's shop and the fruit shop is Aldon Motors' second-hand car lot, who had for sale a ten-year-old Austin A40 Somerset. Parked outside the car lot is a 1958 Sunbeam Rapier II convertible and a Triumph TR4 sports car. (Joe Russell)

In 1962, a young mother pushes her pram to the safety of the pavement at the awkward 'V'-shaped double street junction where Albert and Charles Streets met. The Spon Croft Café was at 303 Oldbury Road on the corner of Albert Street and had formerly been the Five Ways Inn. It had been a beerhouse since at least 1871 and was still in use as pub in the 1930s. Strangely, there had been a Five Ways Café on the western corner of Spon Lane which had been demolished to make way for the 1935 Spon Croft public house. (Joe Russell)

At the junction of Oldbury Road and Spon Lane was the Spon Croft public house. It opened on 7 June 1935 to a design by architects, Wood & Kendrick featuring the then fashionable iron-framed windows. It replaced the Spon Lane Tavern which had been on the opposite side of Spon Lane. It closed in 1995 and was demolished in 1999 when the site was sold to the Hindu Cultural Resource Centre. (M&B Crown Archive)

On 2 July 1938, a UEC ex-Radial truck car stands at the Spon Lane intermediate terminus in Oldbury Road just west of the Spon Croft. The original eighteenth-century building closed in 1935 was located on the Smethwick side of the junction which was replaced by a larger public house on the left behind by the tram. It appears that most of the old pub property was not demolished for a number of years. Until the closure of the single-deck operated B&M tram routes along Spon Lane and Bromford Lane on 17 November 1929, there was a reversing triangle at the Spon Lane junction with Oldbury Road which enabled the trams to reverse back to West Bromwich and also gain access to Tividale Works. (Birmingham Central Reference Library)

Above: Spon Lane was one of the West Midland's earliest industrial areas being first recorded in 1694. It was well known for its foundries and glassworks, which was always sweaty, heavy work in front of fiercely hot open furnaces. The demand for refreshment to replenish the loss of body fluid resulted in Spon Lane having over twenty public houses along its one-mile length, the best known perhaps being the Spon Croft. The entrance to the post-1880s Spon Lane Station was on Spon Lane Bridge, a rather splendid building seemingly perched above the tracks. The iron bridge to the right takes Spon Lane over the Telford main line canal. The goods train travelling towards Birmingham is being hauled by a taper-boilered 2-6-2T locomotive 40172. This type of engine was usually employed as a passenger locomotive. (D.J. Norton)

Below: Spon Lane was one of the original stations opened on 1 July 1852 on the Stour Valley line between Birmingham and Wolverhampton. It was originally located on the other, eastern side of Spon Lane Bridge but was rebuilt in the 1880s. It consisted of an up-and-down side platform with loading bays on the southern side which connected with Chance's glassworks. The entrance gates are beyond the platform ahead of the parked wagons on the left. By June 1957, the time of this view, the station had altered little but was beginning to look a little neglected. It was closed just three years later in 1960. (D.J. Norton)

Travelling along Oldbury Road, West Smethwick on Wednesday 12 April 1939. At the corner of Hawthorn Street is UEC-built car 84, which had arrived in 1929 at West Smethwick depot and worked from there until withdrawn on 30 September 1939. The tram is working on the 86 service to Oldbury which had been taken over from the B&M on 1 April 1928. On the left is the factory of the London Screw Company, who made bolts and nuts, while opposite on the right is Oldbury Road Board School. Going towards Smethwick is a brand new Fordson E83W 10cwt van on West Bromwich trade plates and following the tram is a new Morris Eight car. (H.B. Priestley)

Waiting at the West Smethwick depot entrance triangle of tram tracks for a changeover of the crew on 23 September 1939 is one of the UEC-built tramcars, car 107. Built in 1906, these trams had top-covers from new enabling twenty-eight passengers to be carried on the upper saloon in inclement weather. The depot was located at the extreme west of the Smethwick CBC and the far row of the eighteen late 1880s tunnel-back row of houses behind the tram on the right marked the boundary with Oldbury. Opposite the depot was the famous Chance's Glass Works, the Britannia public house and a row of early eighteenth-century workers' cottages. West Smethwick depot had been opened for steam trams in 1885 and had become the B&M electric car depot in 1903. Eventually it had a capacity for forty-four trams. After the operational closure of the depot on the 30 September 1939, all the 103 surviving 71 class trams were stored on the site, and eventually broken up on the extensive forecourt. (A.N.H. Glover)

The remnants of long-abandoned tram tracks are just visible in Oldbury Road during 1947 as one of the Midland Red's rather strange-looking SOS REDDs speeds past the entrance to the former West Smethwick tram depot. These were the first modern double-deckers to be operated by BMMO, entering service in 1932 and surviving until 1950. The narrow width of the cab and the oddly-shaped front upper saloon panel rather spoilt the looks of this 52-seat body built by Short Brothers. Here 1380, (HA 8005), is working on the B87 service which was the direct descendent of the BCT 87 tram route that was abandoned on 30 September 1939. From that date the replacement bus service to Dudley was always operated by Midland Red. (A.N. Porter)

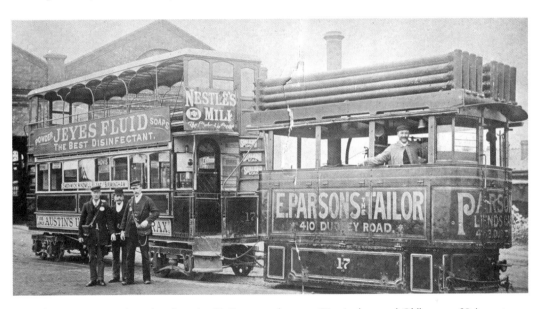

Steam trams were introduced on the 3ft 6in. gauge between Birmingham and Oldbury on 29 August 1885. It was initially an hourly service but soon became every 30 minutes as the service became more popular. The main company depot was a 3½-acre site at West Smethwick about a quarter of a mile to the west of the Spon Lane junction and had a triangle track arrangement which allowed access from Oldbury Road. Standing in front of the impressive car sheds here in 1899 is Kitson locomotive, 17, built in 1886 and rebuilt in 1898 with a three-bay iron cab and Burrell 'cannon'-style condenser mounted on the roof. The innards of these two cylindered 0-4-0 locomotives were always hidden beneath a carriage-like body in which the moustachioed driver is standing. Once underway, the trams waddled and 'hunted' along the tracks which gave them the affection nickname of 'shufflers'. Next to the tram there are two conductors carrying money satchels and a bowler-hatted gentleman, who might be an inspector. Starbucks of Birkenhead built the trailer in 1886, which coincidentally was also numbered 17. This type of bogie trailer, of which this was the first of six, had seating capacities for thirty inside and thirty-two up the outside stairs which, although with top covers, were originally without side 'decency panels'. (H.A. Whitcombe)

West Smethwick depot was rebuilt to accommodate electric trams late in 1903, the work being done by William Bain of Coatbridge. The depot was rebuilt with brick walls and a corrugated iron roof with full-height wooden doors to each of the internal roads. West Smethwick was reopened on 24 November 1904 with eleven tracks each capable of taking four tramcars. Standing in the doors of the car sheds here in June 1938 are eleven UEC-built top-covered ex-Radial truck tramcars which dated from between August 1906 and March 1907. These are, from right to left, four wheel tramcars 129, 195, 153, 94, 107, 151, 136, 193, 192 and 186. The odd man out is the tram on the extreme left which is the recently withdrawn car 490, formerly CBT tram 227, built as an open-top 'Aston'-type by Brush in the winter of 1904. (Birmingham Central Reference Library)

Mr Albert Oakes was a baker at 268 Oldbury Road. He is seen here on his rounds in about 1922. He stands alongside his horse and two-wheeled delivery trap just beyond West Smethwick tram depot, in Oldbury Road. (Joe Russell)

nine

Bearwood

Above: Located at 304 High Street, the Park Hotel, at the junction with Newlands Green, opposite Victoria Park, was by 1902, the time of this photograph, about twenty years old. The architects were the ever-obliging Wood & Kendrick and their building has changed very little externally since. The three lanterns over the entrances are staggeringly large! The original Sow and Pigs public house building used to stand nearby in High Street. (A. Maxam Collection)

Left: The Edward Cheshire District Nurses Home stood at 2 Bearwood Road and was built in 1902. The frontage of the building was a typical Edwardian Arts and Crafts influenced design with a curious mixture of Dutch gables and Tudor mullion windows. Today it is occupied by the Princess Royal Trust Sandwell Carers Centre. (A. Maxam Collection)

The long, almost straight, Cheshire Road disappears towards Church Road. In 1948, unlike today, there were no parked cars obstructing the road. The Victoria Buildings with the Victoria Park post office date from 1907, the same date as the Council House which is almost opposite this junction in Bearwood Hill. Cheshire Road was named after Smethwick's third mayor in 1902-3, Edward Cheshire, who also founded Cheshire's Brewery at Windmill Lane. (A. Maxam Collection)

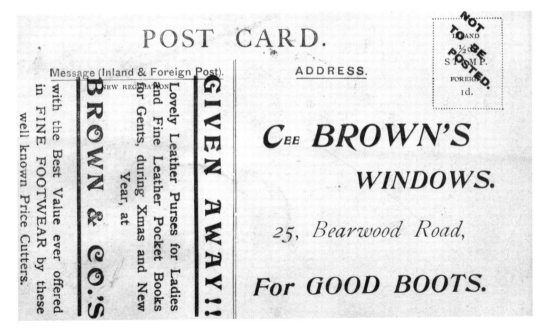

This 1907 postcard was overprinted for J.N Brown & Co., a boot and shoe dealer based at 25 Bearwood Road. They advertised their products with these hand delivered cards, which shows that there is nothing new about cost cutting. (A. Maxam Collection)

Left: The mixture of two- and three-storey terraced houses on the left in Bearwood Road date from the 1890s. Looking from Smethwick towards the Barleycorn public house in about 1910, the houses on the left still overlook open land. Some of these houses have recently been replaced by modern apartments. (A. Maxam Collection)

Below: A panorama taken from the bedroom of one of the houses on Bearwood Road in 1909 shows the Old church and the Old Chapel Inn, which are in the distance in Church Road and The Uplands respectively. The lines of tunnel-back houses in Cheshire and Rosefield Roads were all developed in this decade. (A. Maxam Collection)

Smethwick Old church in Church Road was founded by Dorothy Parkes in 1719. A marble tablet, erected in 1736, commemorating her is on the south wall of the chancel. The chapel, as it was then, was finally consecrated in 1732, becoming the first church in Smethwick. It is a classical building of brick with stone dressings with a west tower and four round-arched windows in the nave. A gallery erected in 1759 now contains the organ. In the church was a clock given in 1932 by Sir John Mitchell who was a member of the local Mitchells brewing family. The vestry, on the northeast, was built in 1963 to replace a smaller one burnt down in 1962. Dorothy Parkes was buried at Harborne in 1728, but her body was moved to Smethwick in 1735. (A. Maxam Collection)

The Old Chapel Inn in The Uplands dates from 1732 and was originally named 'The Hand of Providence In'. In the last part of the nineteenth century it was owned by Cheshire's Brewery. On this sunny summer's day in August 1963, the bowling green at the rear of the pub is through the open gate on the left. The edge of the Old church's churchyard and one of the many memorials is next door to the church, conveying a village atmosphere which looks considerably older than it is. (M&B Crown Archive)

Above: The housing in Wellington Road dates from the last years of the nineteenth century and still survives in 2006. Speeding down the hill from Bearwood Road is a baker's boy on his delivery bicycle. In this part of north Smethwick numerous streets had a mixture of housing styles with terraces, semi-detached houses and large detached villas. (A. Maxam Collection)

Below: Facing towards Smethwick in about 1912 is Arthur Edward Morris's grocer's shop at 268 Bearwood Road. His shop was at the Wellington Road junction and it is an indication of how stable this area was that Mr Morris was still trading over twenty years later. While many of the houses are late Victorian, Capethorn Road, on the right, was only cut in about 1906 on the line of an old field boundary. (A. Maxam Collection)

Right: A fixture list of the Bearwood Harriers for 1909-10 season starts in October and concludes at the end of March. In all twenty-five events were planned, with most of the away fixtures being quite local although they did travel as far as Burton and Coventry. There was a running track in the Oldbury Road area but was this their home track? (A. Maxam Collection)

Below: The elegant and brand-new lounge was the main drinking area of the austere Art Deco-style Barleycorn public house. This was at the junction of Bearwood Road and Dawson Street. This distinctive building opened on 6 April 1939 though a pub had been planned on that site some fifteen years before by architects Wood & Kendrick. At the time of writing, the pub is in danger of being converted into a casino. (M&B Crown Archive)

Bearwood Harriers.

FIXTURES 1909–10.

Oct. 9.	Opening Run	...	...	...	Home
,, 16.	Club Run ...	...	...	...	,,
,, 23.	Paperchase	...	...	...	,,
,, 30.	Walsall H.A.C.	...	...	...	,,
Nov. 6.	Edgbaston H. and Birchfield H.				
	(Selly Oak Branch)	...	...	...	Away
,, 13.	Opening Run at West Bromwich	...	...	Away
,, 20.	Novice Handicap, 5 miles	...	...	Home
,, 27.	Birmingham H.	...	...	...	Away
Dec 4.	Club Run ...	...	...	...	Home
,, 11	,, ,,	...	...	...	,,
,, 18	Edgbaston H.	...	...	...	,,
,, 27.	Paperchase at West Bromwich	...	Away
Jan. 1.	Walsall H.A.C.	...	...	...	,,
,, 8.	Club Run ...	...	...	...	Home
,, 15.	Birmingham H	...	...	...	,,
,, 22.	Club Championship and Sealed Handicap		,,
,, 29.	Club Run ...	...	...	...	,,
Feb. 5.	Midland Counties' Junior Championship			
				Burton-on-Trent
,, 12.	Club Run ...	...	...	...	Home
,, 19.	Novice Championship	...	...	Coventry
,, 26.	Captain v. Vice-Captain Team Race	...	Home
Mar. 5.	5 Mile Handicap	...	...	...	,,
,, 12.	Club Run ...	...	...	...	,,
,, 19.	,, ,,	...	...	...	,,
,, 28.	Outlying Run to Rednall	...	...	,,

Entrance fee to all Club Races and Handicaps 6d., which should be sent in one week before race.

Members Name.....................

Date.....................

Assist. Hon. Sec.:	Hon. Sec.:
A. A. WALPOLE,	W. TIPPETTS,
48, Bishopton Rd., Bearwood.	36, Poplar Rd., Edgbaston.

The Coronation Day of King George V was on 23 June 1911. A street procession passes along Bearwood Road near Marlborough and Talbot Roads. The parade has a large horse-drawn float for a local Mason's Lodge and a banner advertising for a Smethwick-based Friendly Society. (A. Maxam Collection)

Bearwood Road looking towards Smethwick in about 1910 has Beakes Road on the left and Linden Road to the right. Next to Linden Road, the row of shops includes a newsagent and tobacconist's shop and a confectioner just behind 'the boy who moved'. Beakes Road was originally named Franklin Road when first cut in 1903. The row of terraces on the left of Bearwood Road were built in 1879 for Ebenezer Partridge, owner of an engineering works, and this terrace was some of the earliest houses in Bearwood Road, which today are part of the Bearwood Court Hotel. (A. Maxam Collection)

The Coliseum Picture House in Bearwood Road was built in 1911 despite much local opposition. By the late 1920s, it was known as the Bearwood Palais de Danse. By 1931, it was being used by C. Jones & Co. as a furniture store and was later superseded by the nearby Windsor. A petrol station which was later built on the site has now been replaced by modern apartments. (A. Maxam Collection)

The Windsor Theatre, Bearwood Road was built in 1930 at the junction with Dunsford Road and replaced the nearby Coliseum as the local cinema. It had a stage but at first was primarily used as a cinema. After the Second World War it was used as a variety theatre and then it housed a professional repertory company until 1960. (Joe Russell)

The interior of the Bearwood Ice Rink in Bearwood Road shows the upper balcony seating still intact from its days as the Windsor Theatre. The ice rink is seen prior to opening to the public in 1963. Nowadays the building is used as a snooker centre. (Joe Russell)

The tram which is about to cross the junction with Three Shires Oak Road at the Bear Hotel is car 201 and is working on Route B to Bearwood in January 1907 just six months after Birmingham Corporation took over the operation of the service. Three Shires Oak Road, on the left, commemorated the Three Shires Oak tree which marked the boundary of Staffordshire and the detached parts of the counties of Worcestershire and Shropshire. The oak tree was felled in 1904, only months before the B&M opened its Bearwood tramway on 24 November 1904. On the corner of Three Shires Oak Road is G.L. Wheeler's Bearwood Central Fish and Fruit Stores. The buildings on the left of Bearwood Road date from the 1870s and appear to be converted residential properties, while the impressively towered Bearwood Road School was built in 1882. On the right is Sandon Road with larger late Victorian commercial premises on an important corner site. (D.R. Harvey Collection)

Bearwood Road looking towards the Bear Inn. Most of the area around the Three Shires Oak, Bearwood and Sandon Roads junction is already a well-established retail shopping centre, yet even amongst this retail development on the right there were still residential premises in 1912. The only vehicular traffic in Bearwood Road is a horse-drawn baker's delivery van. (A. Maxam Collection)

The Bear Inn, at the junction of Bearwood Road and Three Shires Oak Road, is one of Smethwick's oldest pubs. There has been an inn at this site since at least 1718. The current building was built in 1906 and was constructed several yards back from the previous early nineteenth-century building. This was in order to allow for both road widening and the realignment of the tramlines in Bearwood Road. Today it is part of the Q pub chains, with live music and comedy nights showing that the Bear Hotel is still at the centre of life in Bearwood a century after it was built. (A. Maxam Collection)

The Midland Red FEDD 2368, (FHA 872), is close to moving away from the bus stop in Three Shires Oak Road, with the Bear Hotel and Bearwood Road in the background. No. 2368 is working on the circuitous 229 service to Blackheath through Oldbury and Portway. This bus service included a number of very stiff climbs including those near to Turners Hill. This hill, made up of an outcrop of igneous Rowley Rag, which is a type of dolerite, rises to 876ft and forms part of England's main watershed. (A.B. Cross)

After the 1914 operating agreement with BMMO, Birmingham Corporation was not allowed to run outside the city boundary except in exceptional circumstances. The 6 bus route was introduced on 29 September 1926 and followed the 34 tram route along Hagley Road before turning into Sandon Road. The terminus was in a turning circle at Willow Avenue outside the branch of the Birmingham Municipal Bank. This terminus was barely 100 yards from the Bearwood boundary and only 130 yards from the Bear Hotel at the Bearwood Road and Three Shires Oak Road junction. Looking in pristine condition and still fitted with wheel discs, 2527, (JOJ 527), a Guy 'Arab' III Special 6LW with a Metro-Cammell H30/24R body stands outside the elaborate cast-iron passenger shelter on 16 May 1953 before returning to Birmingham. (J.C. Gillham)

Above: A 1949 Birmingham-registered Austin A40 is parked outside the Rutland Stores at 9 Rutland Road, Bearwood and was an M&B outdoor. In about 1950 it was being run by Edith MacPherson. Above the early 1930s six-light saloon car, on the left, is the roof of the Midland Red bus garage. (M&B Crown archive)

Below: St Mary's church in St Mary's Road, Bearwood was built in 1887 on land given by George Caleb Adkins, the soap industrialist who lived at Lightwoods Hall. He died just before the church was completed. A red-brick Victorian building with Bath stone dressings, it was designed in an Early English style with twelfth century-styled plate tracery windows along the external aisles by J.A. Chatwin of Birmingham. In 1939 the north vestry and parish room were added. It is quite an impressive building that dwarfs the surrounding 1880s terraced housing. (A. Maxam Collection)

Left: From 1903 to 1916, the Revd John Venables was the second vicar of St Mary's church, Bearwood at a time when church attendances were high. The vicarage was built towards the end of his time there and he moved to the South Coast by arranging a swap with the Revd Henry Wynne, the incoming vicar. (A. Maxam Collection)

Below: A lady stands underneath the striped shade of Mary's Wool Shop in St Mary's Road, Bearwood looking at possible purchases. The shop was converted from a row of houses that were built in the late 1880s. She is oblivious to the bus on the 221 service to the Londonderry public house in Norman Road. Passing her by is 2541, (HHA 1), the prototype D1 class bus for the post-war Midland Red bus fleet and entered service in 1945. The body, built by Weymann of Addlestone, was surprising constructed to peacetime Midland Red's specification. This was at a time when buses were still being built to war-time utility designs. The D1 was fitted with rear electric doors in 1949 and from then until its withdrawal in 1961 HHA 1 seemed to be part of Bearwood's furniture as it was always to be seen pottering about the area on one of Midland Red's local services. (A.D. Broughall)

The roadworks in Bearwood Road opposite the junction with St Mary's Road in September 1979 were caused by the building of the new supermarket and shopping centre in Bearwood Road after the Midland Red offices and garage had been demolished. A former Birmingham double-decker, 3438, (438 KOV), a Daimler 'Fleetline' CRG6LX with a Park Royal body dating from 1964, is about to negotiate the road works in Bearwood Road and is being followed by an Austin Princess. (A. Maxam)

The Majestic Cinema was directly opposite St Mary's church in Bearwood Road. In 1928 the Majestic was showing a silent film called *House of Scandal* starring Dorothy Sebastian, who starred in several Buster Keaton films. The Majestic closed in 1958 and became the King's Hall Market until that was demolished in 1981. (A. Maxam Collection)

Wolverhampton District tramcar 10, a 1901 ER & TCW tramcar, follows a horse bus along Bearwood Road and passes St Mary's Road on the left. Tram historians might wonder why this tram was on this route at all. It was either on loan to B&M or it was undertaking some sort of private hire work. Car 10 was a short roof, three side windowed, 45-seater double-decker mounted on American-built Brill 21E trucks and, as if to prove that the tramcar was a 'foreigner', it is displaying advertisements for Bon Marché of Bilston on the rocker panel and for Snape & Sons who were milliners and dressmakers also based in Bilston. (A. Maxam Collection)

Travelling along Bearwood Road in 1965 is 2205, (JOJ 205), which is on the B82 service. It will soon turn right into Anderson Road before terminating in Bearwood bus station. To the left of the bus is Keys Radio shop on the nearer corner of St Mary's Road. On the right, two elderly ladies are walking across the stone sets which marked the entrance to Bearwood garage, with the old Majestic Picture Theatre behind them. 2205 entered service on New Years Day 1950 and spent all but its last few months in service allocated to Rosebery Street garage, being withdrawn on 31 January 1969. (R.F. Mack)

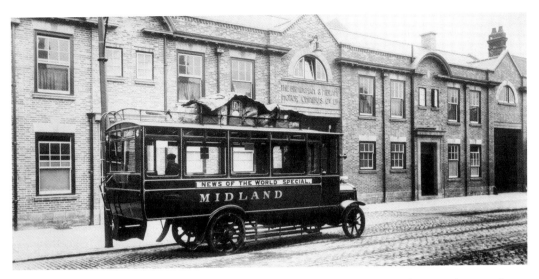

The bus garage in Bearwood Road was the real spiritual home of Midland Red. It was taken over from the CBT tram company on 1 June 1905 and because of congestion at the original Ladywood Road bus garage, all motor bus operation moved into the Bearwood garage on 16 February 1906, but only stayed until October 1907 when all motorised services reverted to horse buses. In October 1914, after the sale of the Birmingham motorbus services to that corporation, along with thirty buses and Tennant Street garage, buses moved back to the renovated Bearwood premises. This single-decker is one of the first motorbuses to be operated by Midland Red after their use was resumed in 1912. In 1915, 0 9939 was being used to deliver the *News of the World* newspaper as part of a distribution contract. (J. Whybrow)

The Birmingham and Midland Motor Omnibus headquarters in Bearwood Road were almost as impressive as the real company name of the bus operator better known as Midland Red. Their four-storey office block dated from 1923 with three large bowed windows set into the Enquiry Office. These bay windows usually displayed scale models of the latest type of Midland Red bus to enter service. A 1936-built SOS FEDD, 1869, (BHA 828), one of a batch of 135 buses was fitted with a metal-framed MCCW H30/26F body, stands outside the Bearwood Road garage entrance awaiting the next driver trainee who will 'try/test his skill' against the 'Silent 3rd' gearbox. The driving school offices were in premises completed in 1935 and which stands in front of 1869. (Omnibus Society)

Speeding along Bearwood Road towards Hagley Road West, with Midland Red's four-storey office block dominating the skyline, is SOS SON single-decker 2052, (DHA 670). This English Electric B38F-bodied bus was built in 1938 and was one of a batch of one hundred. Unlike many SOS buses, their English Electric bodies were not rebuilt during their sixteen-year lifespan. After early withdrawal in 1952, DHA 670 lasted for another four years as one of Bearwood garage's numerous training school buses though it also doubled as a staff bus. The bus has just passed the entrance to Anderson Road with Pooles' furniture store on the corner site and is in front of Edwards's perambulator and toy shop. (A.D. Broughall)

No. 2214, (JOJ 214) was a Leyland 'Titan' PD2/1 with a Park Royal H29/25R body which entered service on 1 February 1950 and survived until 31 July 1969. It spent all but the last year of its service life working from Rosebery Street garage. The outbound buses on the B82 turned into the late Victorian residential heartland of Bearwood from Anderson Road into Herbert Road in order to reach Bearwood bus station. This would have been quite hard work for the driver if he had a 'three-bell' load. There were fifty of these strikingly handsome vehicles, with Rosebery Street being usually allocated the last thirty-four of the class. Although they had BCT interior fixtures and fittings, the buses were a typical product of Park Royal with an 'L'-shape staircase rather than a straight one. (A.B. Cross)

Parked alongside the late Victorian terraces at the Atkins Lane end of Herbert Road, Bearwood is one of the fifty underpowered Metro-Cammell-bodied AEC 'Regent' 0661/20s. Fitted with the AEC 7.58 litre engine, these buses were very heavy, weighing in at just over 7½ tons. The bus has been working on the B82 route from Birmingham when briefly allocated to Oldbury garage. It had entered service in 1950, after a long delay at the bodybuilders, although the chassis had been erected by AEC in 1947 or 1948; 3197, (JHA 98), was withdrawn in 1962. Beyond the newly opened Bearwood bus station is Hagley Road West with its large prestigious late pre-war detached houses. (R.T. Wilson)

Bearwood bus station was opened to traffic on 1 January 1952 although the official opening ceremony took place the following month. The bus station, characterised by its concrete shelters, replaced the termini located around the streets around Bearwood. In the background on the right are the terraced houses in Herbert Road, while dominating the entrance to the bus station and towering over the bus is a huge tree which entering buses had to negotiate. Birmingham City Transport's 2775, (JOJ 775), a Daimler CVD6 with a Metro-Cammell H30/24R body was the last vehicle in the batch of 150 and had entered service on 25 March 1953 and was to survive into West Midlands PTE days, not being withdrawn until 31 March 1971. No. 2775 stands in the bus station in the late summer of 1953 having worked on a B82 service from Birmingham. It is largely in original condition and still sports its wheel discs and trafficators. (D.R. Harvey Collection)

The bus services which replaced the Dudley Road tram routes were jointly operated by BCT and Midland Red, though the B80 to Grove Lane, the B82 to Bearwood and the B83 to Heath Street were the reserve of Birmingham City Transport. The B84 service to St Paul's Road, Smethwick from Edmund Street seemed only to operate on weekdays at 7.00 a.m. and was always operated by BCT. It seems that the service was operated for the early shift workers at Mitchells & Butler's Cape Hill brewery. Conversely the B85 to Spon Lane, the B86 to Oldbury and the B87 to Dudley, which still retained its nickname of 'The Track', were operated by Midland Red from Oldbury garage. No. 2372, (FHA 876), one of the last SOS double-deckers to be delivered in 1939 before the outbreak of the Second World War and fitted with a stylish-looking Brush forward entrance 56-seater body, stands alongside a Leyland-bodied Leyland of the 1953 LD8 class, in Bearwood bus station on Sunday 14 August 1955. (W.A. Camwell)

Midland Red also operated the 233 bus service from Bearwood bus station. It ran a half-hourly service to the George in Warley, to the Plough at Bristnall Fields, to the Hen and Chickens at Causeway Green and then through Langley to the bus station outside the Council House in Oldbury. 4734, (734 BHA), a 1957-vintage BMMO D7 with an MCCW H37/26R body, unloads its passengers having just arrived in Bearwood bus station. On the distant bus stand are two West Bromwich Corporation buses. The rear one, a Daimler CVG6 with an MCCW 'Orion'-type body from the dozen SEA-registered batch of buses, is working on the 221 joint service back to West Bromwich. (R. Weaver)

Standing in the grounds of Lightwoods Park on the border of Bearwood and Birmingham is Lightwoods House. It was built in 1791 for the Leicestershire maltster Jonathan Grundy, who named his new house Lightwoods after the nearby woodland. The house is constructed of brick with stone dressings and stucco decorations added in the nineteenth century. The family remained in the house until 1865 when it was sold for £8,700 to George Caleb Adkins, the local Smethwick-based soap and red-lead manufacturer. In 1902, after the death of his son, property developers were interested in continuing the rapid wedge-shaped growth of 1880s

and 1890s urbanisation across Adkins Lane to the then named Beech Lanes, which would have meant demolishing Lightwoods House. Although the house and grounds were put up for sale, Alexander Macomb Chance, one of the Chance glassmaking family of Spon Lane, purchased the estate for £13,000 and donated it to Birmingham Corporation who turned the gardens into a public park with a large ornamental pool. This intensely political move effectively blocked the southern housing expansion of Bearwood to the Beech Lanes boundary. (D.R. Harvey Collection)

This postcard view shows Lightwoods Park with the abbey, sundial and rose gardens at Warley Park, together with the hall, tennis courts and Edwardian bandstand with its delicate wrought-iron work. Here also was the famous Shakespeare Garden, which grew all the flowers and plants mentioned in the Bard's plays. Both Lightwoods and Warley Parks, although lying within Smethwick's boundaries, were administered for many years by Birmingham. (A. Maxam Collection)

During the last two decades of the nineteenth century Bearwood's development was centred on Bearwood Road, which linked the Hagley Road-Beech Lanes junction at the Old King's Head with the Sandon Road-Three Shires Oak Road junction at the even older Bear Inn. Bearwood had originally been part of the Parish of Harborne, but in 1888 joined Smethwick in not agreeing to become part of Birmingham. The result was that Bearwood Road was hemmed in to the west by the Warley boundary and to the east by Birmingham's boundary leaving Bearwood Road and its surrounding streets as a wedge between the two other authorities. The 1880s housing development along Bearwood Road therefore rapidly changed from a residential one into the main shopping area for Bearwood. In this transition period in about 1910, BCT tramcar 179 stands at the Bearwood terminus. The tramcar is has open platforms and vestibules and it carries the stencil 'B' on a black ground to show that it is on the Bearwood to Edmund Street service. Poplar Road is on the right with a beer-seller's shop retailing the locally brewed Cheshires Ales.

Below: Smethwick was created a County Borough in 1907 and began issuing the well-known HA registration on 1 April 1907. The HA registration was made famous after 1920 as all Midland Red

buses were registered in Smethwick. On 1 April 1966 Smethwick was incorporated into the new Warley CB who continued to issue the HA until somewhat confusingly the letters were transferred to Dudley in the same year as Smethwick ceased to be an independent borough. New signs began to appear in 1974 advertising the fact that Smethwick was now part of Sandwell MBC. By 1978, one such sign had been erected in Bearwood Road.
(A. Maxam)

In the summer of 1952, 2489, (JOJ 489), waits alongside the 1905-built Kings Head public house in Lordswood Road while the crew stand alongside the Bundy Clock. The bus is within sight of Bearwood Road's shops and Bearwood bus station which are about 100 yards away to the rear of the bus. The bus is a Crossley DD42/6 with a Crossley H30/24R body. The bus entered

service on 1 July 1950 and after having spent most of its life at Harborne garage was sold for preservation in September 1969 and has been inactive ever since. (D.R. Harvey)

The southern boundary of Bearwood with Birmingham was along the centre of Beech Lanes, later to become Hagley Road West. Facing Birmingham, on 19 March 1972, 2966, (JOJ 966), a 1953-vintage Guy 'Arab' IV, is working on the 9 route from Quinton. It is in the bus lay-by alongside Lightwoods Park and Bearwood bus station. On the corner of Bearwood Road is the Royal Liver Friendly Societies' office in the late nineteenth-century block of twenty-five individual premises in the Bearwood side of Hagley Road. Opposite is the Kings Head public house. The original Old Kings Head was a Georgian inn on the Birmingham to Halesowen road and was replaced by the new building in 1905 to the designs of Messrs Owen and Ward, who were also responsible for the splendid Hare and Hounds in Kings Heath. The outside is a fairly typical Arts and Crafts-inspired mixture of brick, terracotta and half timbering set off with pinnacles. The original interior was a wonderful extravagance of brown and green Maws tiles. The Kings Head is to the right of the former BCT Guy 'Arab' IV 3080, (MOF 80), which was by now owned by West Midlands PTE. (E.V. Trigg)

The contrast between large detached inter-war houses on the Birmingham side of Hagley Road West and the Bearwood side of the main road to Halesowen could not have been greater. The northern side of Hagley Road consisted of the wide open spaces of Lightwoods Park which went across to Adkins Lane and Lightwoods Hill some 250 yards away. Storming up the hill away from the Kings Head on its way to Wolverhampton is a most unusual pre-war single-decker. No. 1668, (AHA 612), was one of twenty-five SOS OLR normal control coaches with a canvas-roof 29-seater bodies which were designed in 1935 for summer touring. During the Second World War these coaches were redundant as coach operation was suspended for the duration. These OLRs were rebuilt by Midland Red to forward control 34-seater buses; 1668 was rebuilt in 1941 and remained in service until 1951. (A.N. Porter)

Originally dating back to the 1830s, the Cock & Magpies pub was in Beech Lanes which was the main road to Halesowen and Stourbridge. In later years this road was renamed Hagley Road West. The pub was rebuilt in the inter-war period but the interior was extensively rebuilt during the mid-1960s. Shortly after it was first reopened in November 1967, the lounge already had a dated appearance. In 2000 the Cock and Magpies became a Harvester restaurant. (M&B Crown Archive)

ten

Thimblemill Road, Abbey Road and Warley

Church of
Our Lady of
Good Counsel
and
Saint Gregory,
Bearwood.

✠

Architect's Sketch.

An architect's sketch by P.B. Chatwin of Birmingham shows the Roman Catholic church of Our Lady of Good Counsel and St Gregory. This church was built at Three Shires Oak Road, Bearwood in 1933-34 though it was not consecrated until 1961. It was built in the style of a third-century Roman Basilican church, but it still looked like a 1930s-building. (A. Maxam Collection)

At the corner junction of Abbey Road with Thimblemill Road was The Abbey public house. A petition by local residents had ensured that it wasn't built in 1920 when it was first proposed and so it was eventually opened on 2 October 1931 and here in 1967 it still looks in remarkably original condition. Originally it was to be called The Castle. The architects were Wood & Kendrick of West Bromwich who worked on many M&B public houses in the 1920s and 1930s. (M&B Crown Archive)

Children enjoy the school fayre and other outdoor activities in the playground of St Gregory's RC Primary School when it was first opened in 1968. The new school was located between Park Road and Wigorn Road, Bearwood. (Joe Russell)

Thimblemill Baths was built between Reginald Road and Gladys Road on Thimblemill Road and is still in use here as one of the best swimming pools in the West Midlands, having been extended in 1966. The blocks of flats in Thimblemill Road also date from the 1930s and have a vaguely municipal Art Deco style. They are behind Midland Red's 1483, (HA 9380), which was a 1934 SOS BRR with a Short B34F body with an exaggeratedly high saloon roof-line. The bus still has a small Second World War, military-type nearside headlight. (D.R. Harvey)

Smethwick Swimming Baths in Thimblemill Road were opened in 1933 in order to relieve pressure on Rolfe Street Baths, which had been opened in 1888 and survived until 1989 when they were dismantled brick-by-brick and reconstructed at the Black Country Living Museum. Originally Thimblemill Road Baths had one swimming pool, twenty-four slipper baths and a café lounge. When not in use the pool could be covered over and used as either an auditorium or a public hall, having a large stage area located behind the removable diving board. In the 1950s the baths were used for international swimming competitions. (A. Maxam Collection)

The Thimble Mill Inn was built at 174 Thimble Mill Road on the corner with Norman Road to the designs of architects Wood & Kendrick. It opened on 5 April 1928 just five days after this part of Oldbury became incorporated into Smethwick CBC. The Thimblemill was built to cater for the new residents of the local 1920s and 1930s suburban expansion in this part of Bearwood. On this snowy day in 1963 the pub seems to have a reasonably full car park with, including the van, no less than four Austin A35s. (M&B Crown Archive)

Although Norman Road had been cut in 1907 it was only after the end of the First World War that any speculative private housing developments began. Municipal houses began to be constructed at the end of the Twenties and by 1935 Smethwick's 4,000th council house was opened, thus achieving the target which the Council had set for its housing programme back in 1920. To mark the occasion, a brick sundial was unveiled. Norman Road is one of several in the area, such as Rathbone, Sydney and Hamilton, named after family members of industrialist William Henry Jones. The parked car is a 1927 Jowett Long-Four Tourer. (A. Maxam Collection)

No. 3813, (NHA 813) is a BMMO D5B with a solidly built 'heavyweight' metal-framed body built by Brush. With a BMMO 8.028 litre Diesel engine and an all-up weight of just under 8 tons, the D5Bs, the first buses in the fleet to have rear platform doors, gave a comfortable ride for its passengers. It is leaving Bearwood on the 221 service to West Bromwich, but the destination blind has not been rewound. The bus is near the top of the steady climb up Lightwoods Hill near to Warley Woods at the junction with Harborne Road on the right. (A.D. Broughall)

Approaching the bus stop in Thimblemill Road opposite Thimble Mill Pool is a Midland Red 2162, (EHA 294), a Brush-bodied SOS FEDD dating from 1938, which is working on the 121 service from Langley to Birmingham via Londonderry and Bearwood. This bus was nearing the end of its working life being withdrawn in 1958. Thimble Mill Pool had become part of an area of open space later used as a recreation park. Originally it served as the water supply for a medieval corn mill, and during in the eighteenth century it became a thimble making workshop, hence the name of the road. Behind and above the bus is a typical 1930s municipal semi-detached house which was so typical of the Smethwick area. (A.D. Broughall)

A Scout Jamboree took place at Warley Woods on Saturday 9 July 1910. A large Edwardian open tourer is being used as a vantage point. On the right is a large marquee being used as a refreshment tent. Businessman Samuel Galton purchased the Warley Hall Estate in 1792 and employed landscape architect Humphrey Repton to lay out the park. Galton, of bridge fame, had built in 1819 the mock-Gothic pile of Warley Abbey which was unfortunately demolished in 1957. The park was saved from development in 1906 when it donated to Birmingham City Council and subsequently opened to the public. It is now administered by the Warley Woods Community Trust. (A. Maxam Collection)

Barclay Road, with Warley Woods visible on the left, commemorates the marriage of Samuel Galton junior to Lucy Barclay, a member of the Quaker family that founded Barclay's Bank. These deceptively large houses were still quite new just before the First World War and exhibited a vaguely Arts and Crafts look. (A. Maxam Collection)

Pupils pose for the camera at Abbey Road Junior and Infants School, possibly for an Empire Day celebration. The school was built in 1909 in a typical Board-School style and was officially opened the following year with a capacity for 1,140 children. For many years in the summer months, some lessons took place at nearby Warley Woods. (A. Maxam Collection)

Other local titles published by Tempus

Central Birmingham Pubs Volumes I and II

JOSEPH MCKENNA

These volumes record the pubs, inns, taverns and beerhouses of the central city, an area now within the present Inner Ring Road and the Bull Ring. Although only one mile square, it is an area that has seen over 760 pubs – all of which are faithfully recorded here. These books are a valuable account of the history of Birmingham's pubs – the people who ran them, the customers who frequented them and the brewers who supplied and usually owned them. Take a 'pub crawl' and explore the social and historical functions of the public houses in this area.

0 7524 3873 5 / 0 7524 4144 2

Dudley

DAVID CLARE

This fascinating collection highlights some of the changes and developments that have taken place in Dudley over the last 150 years. Originally a medieval market town, Dudley was shaped by the Industrial Revolution and occupied an integral place at the heart of the Black Country. Every aspect of Dudley is explored, from the people and buildings of this strong community to market days, transport and shops; from the highest tower of the castle to the subterranean limestone caverns beneath Castle Hill.

0 7524 3534 5

Handsworth Volume II

MARIA TWIST

This collection of over 200 photographs, many from the archives of the Central Birmingham Library, takes the reader on a pictorial journey around Handsworth from the 1870s to the 1980s, exploring the streets and the churches, the houses, public buildings and schools. With archive images of the Soho Manufactory, the Handsworth Carnival and the town's beautiful park, this nostalgic collection will appeal to all who know the area.

0 7524 3358 X

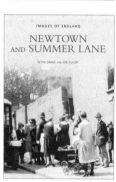

Newtown and Summer Lane

PETER DRAKE AND JON GLASBY

References to Summer Lane and Newtown are rarely seen in published accounts yet this area, close to the city centre, was a densely occupied one, and one that inspired strong local loyalties. After the Second World War, during which the area sustained considerable bomb damage, a programme of slum clearance and redevelopment took place. This collection will be an important record for those who have lived and worked in the area and will put on the historical map an area that has until now been largely neglected by historians.

0 7524 4197 9

If you are interested in purchasing other books published by Tempus, or in case you have difficulty finding any Tempus books in your local bookshop, you can also place orders directly through our website

www.tempus-publishing.com